HOW TO NOT F$$$K UP

YOUR FINANCIAL FUTURE
AND THE REST OF YOUR LIFE

*"You can be more successful than your parents
and peers, and live a better life."*

A book by **Louis Berlin**
Financial, Business, and Personal Mentor

Wharton School of Finance, MBA 1977
Princeton University, BA 1975

ISBN: 978-1-7241-9514-2

Cover Design by Enid Nolesco
Interior layout by Velin Saramov

Printed in the United States of America

CONTENTS

CONTENTS

WHY READ THIS BOOK

You NEED TO THINK OF your life as a business.

Because it is a business—"The (insert your name here) Company"

It is this business that is going to determine how well you live while you are working, and how well you are going to live after you stop working.

Billionaire investor Warren Buffet once said, "Never invest in a business you cannot understand."

You need to understand how your finances work, and how you can effectively manage them and take control. You need to understand what you need to do to be extremely successful. And you need to understand who and what is getting in your way.

In this book, you are going to learn:

- How to be your own primary financial advisor
- How to make the best financial decisions, independent of advertising
- How to make plans to reach your goals
- How to evaluate financial choices
- How to understand your options, and the products are offered to you
- How to seek out the best solutions for yourself

You are also going to learn something no other finance book will teach you:

- How to evaluate people who are trying to sell you something
- How to be the most successful person you can be

The goal is for you to become more successful than your parents and peers, and live a better life.

INTRODUCTION

WOULDN'T YOU LIKE TO KNOW how to make decisions—financial, business and personal—that are rational and based on facts, and not feelings?

Wouldn't you like to make those decisions confidently?

Your success in life—both personally and professionally—is highly dependent on the skills you develop to think and feel independently.

Your financial success depends in a large part on your ability to sort through all the misleading and manipulative information in the marketplace so you can arrive at decisions that are good for you. You need to make financial decisions without having to rely on salespeople, advertising, and other self-serving interests.

But you need more than just good information—you need to be able to process information free of your personal biases, and independent of marketplace attempts to manipulate you.

I take an unusual, and perhaps unique, approach to developing financial security. I focus simultaneously on the inner forces that direct your thinking as well as on the outside information you receive.

And when you no longer have the continual to worry about finances, you will spend more time enjoying life and reaching your highest potential.

Consider this:

Amassing money and making it grow depends on the skills you develop. Part of this skill set is influenced by the factors in your upbringing that you bring with you into adulthood. And part is influenced by how you process information from the marketplace. There is tremendous pressure from marketers to get you to spend money, and tremendous pressure from the investment and financial community to turn your money over to them for management. The marketing community (financial and otherwise) knows exactly how to push your buttons to get you to part with your money.

But, ultimately, you need to take responsibility for managing your financial future.

Most of this book focuses on finances and insurance. But at certain points, we are going to focus on you as a human being as well. Because how well you know yourself will impact on how well you can make financial decisions. Throughout this book you will get glimpses of how to progress in this ongoing life effort. Eventually, you will be extremely successful as a result of finding teachers and mentors who are willing to share both their successes and struggles. And once you master your personal decision-making process, you will grow in confidence and embrace what I call your "awesomeness."

You have the potential for personal success and financial comfort, but you must focus on both areas for maximum results. One influences the other. It takes self-confidence and the ability to access knowledge to resist market forces that seek to take advantage of you and your finances. Without financial security and confidence, it is hard to pursue personal success.

Making good decisions is EASY to do when you follow the basic rules you will learn here, and that will put you in a solid financial position. You will be better off than your parents, and better off than your peers.

I want you to get answers to questions you ask yourself, such as:

- How do I save and budget money?
- What questions do I have to ask to make sure I've covered all the important financial topics?
- How do I manage assets efficiently?
- How do I evaluate advice impartially?
- How do I make sure I have enough money to fund the lifestyle I want?
- How do I make sure I don't run out of money?
- How do I recognize and deflect tactics meant to take advantage of me?

I want you to learn about the people and companies that sell you financial products, how to separate the bullshit and schemes from valuable information, and how to avoid the uneducated advisors and just plain unethical people who will gladly lead you down the wrong financial path for their own gain.

I want you to learn how to not mess up your financial future and the rest of your life.

One area I want to make you stronger in is dealing with the poorly educated but well-meaning advisors, who have succumbed to industry propaganda, who end up misleading you due to their own ignorance, and not because they have bad intent. These types of "advisors" are the ones you have to be especially alert for, because they are so sincere, so well meaning, and so deluded that they do not realize how much damage they are doing. They are extremely persuasive, and they really believe in what they are doing. And you may willingly abdicate scrutiny of their recommendations because you are not confident in your own abilities in the unfamiliar area of finances. I want to change that.

I also want you to understand my personal biases, to be able to independently evaluate what I say and suggest.

Here is a true story that shows the skills I want you to have by the time you are done reading this book:

I met recently with Dave, a new acquaintance, so we could learn more about each other's business. In the course of the conversation, I explained how I often helped people evaluate insurance policies they owned, and what some of the problems I found. His face started to lose color, and he confided that early that same day he had taken delivery of, and paid for, two insurance policies that he applied for a month earlier, before we had met each other. Apparently, I was triggering some doubts.

About a year before, he had purchased a policy from a salesperson who was also a friend, and who worked for company A. He was under the impression that this policy would perform a certain way, and require a certain premium, that would never change. Whether he came to this conclusion on his own, or was misdirected (i.e. " lied to") by the salesman is not certain. (However, I've seen this before from company A's people, and I strongly suspect the latter.)

About a month prior to our meeting, he ran into another friend, from Company N, who pointed out the problems with Company A's policy. Dave surrendered Company A's policy, at a loss, and purchased two policies from Company N.

Now he was having doubts about the two new policies, based on what I was telling him. He ran to his car, grabbed the two new policies, and brought them for us to review jointly. And sure enough, he had been taken advantage again—not only was one not going to perform as advertised, but the other was way more expensive than other similar policies he could have purchased, from other companies, that would perform identically.

In addition to being angry, he also said that he felt that "he was made to feel stupid" and that, as a highly intelligent professional with an advanced degree, he "should have been able to better evaluate the information he was given and the products he was buying."

My job now became more than just teaching him about insurance. Now, I had to remind him that:

- no one can make him feel stupid without his consent,
- that it is unreasonable for him to think that by virtue of his expertise in his own, complex professional field, he should also be an expert in evaluating insurance policies, which is an equally complex, but different, field, and
- by maintaining a healthy dose of skepticism about salespeople and sales tactics, and learning how to independently process information, he can make good decisions.

I want you to learn how to do this for yourself. The key to being better off financially and personally is to start NOW, no matter how old you are. Assets and money compound over time. The earlier you stash money away, and the better you manage it, the more wealth you will have later on.

Start your journey toward personal success now by learning about:

- Building on what you've already learned
- Increasing what you learn from others
- Experiencing setbacks and losses
- Realistically looking at the messages you give yourself—the positive ones that push you ahead and reinforce your strengths, and the negative ones that hold you back.

(Some of the information in this book will be familiar to readers of my two prior books, "The Financial Fitness Handbook" (2011) and "Financial Fitness for Everyone" (2016), which have both been updated. A majority of this book is new material.)

WHAT I DO, AND WHO I AM

I was born in 1953, the first child of Lila and George Berlin, and lived in a tiny apartment in Manhattan for six months, until my father bought a $15,000, two-bedroom, one-bath starter home in the suburbs. Mom worked as a nurse until I was born and then retired to take care of what would quickly become a family of four. Dad, a Navy vet and college-trained civil engineer, began a fifteen-year career in a concrete supply company, thinking he would be there forever. Growing up, I often spent weekends with Dad, hosing the chutes of concrete trucks before the tailings could harden. After the concrete company went bankrupt, and the owners forged papers saying that Dad had an ownership position so as to try to saddle him with their liabilities, I figured out that financial security in building something of my own, and not working for others.

Mom's youth had been colored by the Depression. Her father was often out of work, and her mother struggled to provide for the four girls (the only viable births from seven pregnancies, which also produced two stillborn babies and a short-lived son). As a teenager, Mom sold sandwiches by the roadside, near a farm that relatives lived on for a while, and then, back in Manhattan, went door-to-door selling subscriptions. The fear of not having food or money became ingrained into her subconscious, and I clearly remember bringing a sack lunch to school, every day, with three pennies to buy a half-pint of milk. Rarely was there an extra nickel for a candy bar, although an extra nickel a day, $13 a year, would not have taxed the family budget (even if all four children got that nickel). A cafeteria hot lunch for thirty-five cents was achieved but once or twice a year. Suffice it to say, with the school lunch program being my Holy Grail of gourmet food, the first time I went to an all-you-can-eat buffet restaurant, I thought I had died and gone to Heaven. (Who knows what damage I have inflicted on my children by making them eat what was in the refrigerator, irrespective of its age or state of decay?)

The lesson I learned from vicariously living Mom's youth was that, if I did not provide for myself, I might indeed go hungry in the future.

I began my working career in 3rd grade, publishing a short-lived, one-page community newspaper, which Mrs. Shepard, my teacher, was gracious enough to make mimeo copies of at school. I attempted to peddle these door to door for three cents a copy, but the smell of the acetone toner brought back too many memories of surprise quizzes and worksheets that my potential customers had endured in childhood, and they did not sell.

Since then, I've been involved in over thirty businesses, sometimes as an employee, but more often as an owner and entrepreneur, generally with a partner or two, and the success or failure of my efforts depended mainly on my wits, determination, incredibly long work day, fear of failure, and luck. These forty-plus years of my adult working life have brought me a wealth of experience and insight into human behavior, and a clear understanding of what it takes to succeed. They have also taught me just how ill prepared we all are for a life of financial peace of mind. Too much is invested in hopes and dreams, and wishing that things will turn out a certain way, at the expense of realistic planning.

A number of years ago, I turned to the world of insurance and finance, in part because, amidst the joys of life, several unpleasant surprises and tragic events occurred:

- My mother-in-law spent twenty-seven years flat on her back in a nursing home, supported by Medicaid. Several state employees began their careers in the Department of Family Services with Jane's case already open, and they retired before it was closed. She may well have been the longest case on record.
- My sister-in-law, age 61, was hit by a car, thrown twenty-five feet, broke everything, was in a coma for three months, and was still in rehab over eighteen months later. She had no disability or long-term care insurance.
- My Dad passed away. He was woefully under-insured, and some of the insurance he had was totally inappropriate.
- My Mom's long-term care insurance lapsed, leaving her with annual costs in excess of $100,000, and a lifetime cost of $1,500,000.
- Some investments I had were tied to the stock market, which tanked just when I needed the money.
- It turned out that some wildly popular insurance products that I owned were invested in the stock market as well.
- I discovered that I had reached middle-aged, which was quite a surprise, because I had been thinking that I was still young.

Reviewing insurance was never on my list of top ten things to do. I did not like shopping for insurance. And I thought growing old was something that would happen in the future. But after I reviewed my policies a while ago, I concluded that I was missing important coverage, paying for policies that were no longer right for me, and not getting the most out of the good policies that I owned. So I took matters into my own hands; I went to school and got a license to sell insurance. Then, I fixed my policies that were worth saving, cancelled the others, and added some new ones that I needed. It occurred to me that I might not be alone, so I started talking to people. It turns out that I was right. I have yet to find anyone who likes shopping for insurance, and I've collected a set of insurance horror stories. I turned what I learned into a career—and you can save time and money and benefit from my learning just by talking to me.

I approach insurance the way I approach everything else—studying, gaining knowledge, and seeking out mentors with experience and the proper connections. And I listen to people's needs. That's what I was taught at Princeton University, and at the Wharton School of Finance, while studying for my MBA. (It's also what I taught my undergraduate students there, while I was getting my MBA.) It's the methodology I've used to build several successful businesses. It's the bedrock of my ability to help people achieve financial peace of mind.

In the philanthropic world, I have started and developed several charities, with a strong focus on child abuse, poverty, and teaching life-enhancing values. I support numerous organizations, including serving on local, national, and international boards. I have developed several successful programs that I use when training and teaching.

I particularly enjoy mentoring others to live more successful, prosperous, and inspired lives. As an author, lecturer, and teacher, I have addressed the issues of success in business, financial, personal, and philanthropic arenas. By improving and transforming the quality of life for others, I have earned the trust, respect, and a continuing business of individuals, groups, businesses, and non-profits.

"What is your work?" someone asked me recently. It took me a while to answer, because I am usually asked "What do you do for a living?" and the response is easy—I sell insurance and financial products, and the insurance companies pay me a commission or fee, which provides the bulk of my income, or "living."

"What is my work?" however, is a different question, because my work does not always provide me a living. I see my work as basically listening to people, hearing their hopes and dreams and concerns, answering questions about money and risk, and helping them figure out what steps they need to take to achieve those goals, while protecting themselves financially against obstacles that may get in the way.

My work is learning about all parts of their lives—about the people they love, about the people they are financially responsible for, about the people who help them, about the people who might try to take advantage of them, about the people and situations that expose them to risk. A lot of my time is spent advising on things that I have learned the hard way—business relationships, child rearing, relationship building, self-confidence, marketing, negotiating, getting an idea across to others. My work is teaching what experience and people have taught me. None of this generates income. A lot of my time is spent explaining the myriad of alternatives for investing, saving, building assets, reducing liabilities, managing money, etc.—for which I often refer people to other professionals, and for which I do not get paid. More often than not, I can help these people acquire insurance and some other financial products that are an essential part of the risk reduction/income production/asset preservation balance.

From this part of my work, I make my living. I also help people with mortgages and property insurance—anything that can save them money on big-ticket items— because there is a lot of money they can save if I do the right thing for them. And I mentor people one on one—to help them personally, to help them professionally, and to help their businesses grow.

PART I:

HOW TO APPROACH YOUR FINANCIAL DECISIONS

Chapter 1

WHERE ARE YOU NOW, FINANCIALLY?

No MATTER HOW OLD YOU are, you can improve your financial future now.

Are you the parent of a child, who is not able to read yet, with no income? Good. Maybe Grandma even reads "Goodnight, Moon" to your child while living the story of "Goodbye, Money?" You'll be surprised to learn that there are things you can do for your child or grandchild, who has no money, to get started on creating a great financial future.

Are you a teenager, in high school? Great—you are going to learn how to avoid debt so that you won't have problems after school (and the rest of your life).

Are you coming out of college? Do you have debt, or did you survive debt free? Doesn't matter—we'll work with each scenario.

Married? Partnered? Thinking about it? No kids yet? All of these are awesome times. You can do tremendous damage, or tremendous good. Your financial success for the next seventy years is going to be highly predicated upon decisions you make today. I'll explain why, in very easy to understand terms.

Do you have children? Thinking about buying a house? Beyond the stage of "having a job" and into "the beginning of a career"? Way to go! Dealing with debt from earlier years? No problem! Debt free? Even better!

Middle aged? You need to act fast, but there is a lot you can do.

Pre-retirement? Okay—time is working against you, but your life experiences and whatever you've built up is working for you. With this in mind, you can't afford to make a bad move. You have to act deliberately with a lot of forethought, because at this stage, it is actually easier to see what the financial future looks like, as compared to when you were younger. The choices are fewer, the risks need to be less, and the outcomes will be more certain.

Retired? Piece of cake! Let's get going, and make precise, educated moves that will guarantee that your money lasts your entire lifetime, and then some.

I want to wish you happy birthday 20, 30, and even 40 years from now, with the full knowledge that the plans you made have come to fruition and that you are financially secure for the rest of you life.

If you have not made any plans, that is a plan in and of itself, and that plan is for financial security to happen only by chance. It is not a good plan, and it is the one that most people in my generation, and your parents' generation, used. You know how most of us are doing—it is not a position you want to be in yourself.

If you are between 25 and 34 years old, we want to look at a forty-year horizon. You may still be paying off education loans; you may or may not have entered a permanent relationship; you may or may not have started raising children; and you may or may not have honed in on a career. Financially, you are still experimenting and taking chances. It sounds confusing because it is confusing. I use the term "may or may not" a lot, because things are continually in a state of flux. I use the term "permanent" loosely, because what you think is permanent now—relationships, career, or passions—may still change, and you are well aware of that. It is good that we have a forty-year horizon, because we need more time—both to get to a stable base and to build, allowing for chances of setbacks and change. If you have student debt, it is hanging over year head and clouding your vision. Your primary thought at this time is probably how to get rid if it. That is only half the battle. If you simply get rid of debt in ten to twenty years, all you are is debt-free, which means you have no assets, and fewer income earning years ahead of you. This means that you will not have enough money in later years or that you will be in debt, again, later in life, when you no longer have the prospect of paying it back. The decisions you make now must address both issues simultaneously: clearing up debt and amassing wealth.

If you are between 35 and 44 years old, we want to look at a thirty-year horizon. You should be most, or all, of the way through your debt repayment years, perhaps into raising children, looking at incurring new debt for their schooling, and have already stocked away some money for retirement and/or custodial care in your later years. The decisions you want to make now involve reviewing what you've saved so far, and making firm, long-term choices that will produce certain and desirable outcomes.

If you are 45 to 54 years old, we have a twenty-year horizon. This means we have to act quickly and decisively on cleaning up your remaining financial challenges, proceeding with utmost certainty and caution, because twenty years is when we will just begin to see the substantive returns on the plans we enact now.

If you are over 55 and not yet financially secure you need specific, immediate plans and actions. You should be meeting with several people like me to decide who can help you best. If you are financially secure, both for now and the future, you should probably be focusing on helping the two generations after you. The focus is going to be on how you can simultaneously protect what you have, and keep control of your assets, while simultaneously laying the groundwork for your grandchildren to get a twenty or thirty year head start on financial security.

Your next step is to assess where you are right now, and where you were a year ago. If you do not know this, you cannot measure progress. If you do not know where you've been and where you are going, you cannot tell where you are heading, or where you will end up. To know if you are "there" yet, you need to know what "there" looks like. And if you don't know what "here" looks like, you have no way to track progress. If you cannot track progress, and do not know what the destination looks like, who knows where you'll end up, or if that is where you even want to be.

We need to get to work.

Chapter 2

HOW TO PLAN TO TAKE ADVANTAGE OF GOOD OPPORTUNITIES WHEN THEY COME YOUR WAY

WELL THOUGHT-OUT PLANS ARE GOOD to have and to use as a guide. But they have to be flexible, allowing you to alter your direction, or change it entirely. The greatest financial successes will always come from serendipity—you'll be in a certain place, at a certain time, an opportunity will present itself, and you'll be positioned to take advantage of it. It will just fall in your lap.

For example, my brother-in-law was appointed trustee for his late uncle's estate in 2008, which included an apartment in a part of town I was unfamiliar with. While cleaning out the apartment, we saw the potential of the apartment, and the neighborhood, and we made the acquaintance of a neighbor, David, who was a real estate broker. We bought the apartment from the estate, at a fair market value, and we wanted to invest in more apartments in the neighborhood. So we told David to keep an eye out for opportunities to buy. And sure enough, during the 2009 real estate crash the following year, a bank to help sell a nearby apartment that it had foreclosed on enlisted David.

He dutifully put it up for sale and gave us notice that it was being posted on the Internet at noon. By 2 p.m., we had seen the unit and written a full-price offer. By 3 p.m., we faxed the offer to the bank, and they signed it at 4 p.m., contingent on us getting a $32,000 cashier's check to them within 24 hours. I had next to nothing in the bank, and there was no place to get that money fast since banks were not lending. Therefore, I called my whole life insurance company, ordered an advance on the cash value in my policy, and had them overnight a check to the seller. We rented the apartment for a year, and then sold it for $80,000, resulting in a profit of $48,000. In one year.

I didn't plan for the real estate crash, and I didn't plan to hear about this great opportunity. I was just lucky it all fell into place. Yet I was also prepared. I had readily available financial resources because I had planned to be ready to take advantage of opportunities, without even knowing what those opportunities would be.

The key here was not only having put aside the resources and having made them grow in the years leading up to this opportunity, but also in having the knowledge to be able to evaluate the opportunity. It also meant being confident enough in my preparation and education to quickly act to move forward when others were scared or foolish.

Let's go back to my brother-in-law's uncle's apartment. His uncle had lived in it for 40 years. It was a mess. He hoarded everything. He had never fixed it up. The kitchen and bathroom had old, outdated broken fixtures and appliances. There was so much junk stacked up in the bedrooms that we were not even sure if there were walls and windows in some areas. But when we cleaned it out (2 dumpsters worth of trash) and tore out the kitchen and the carpets, we realized we had a gem. It would have been hard to sell to anyone else before we cleaned it up, because it was hard to see the potential.

What about the $32,000 apartment? This unit had been purchased a few years before, at the height of the housing bubble, and when the bank foreclosed, the amount owed, in principal and interest, was over $230,000. The people who had bought it, and then defaulted, had overpaid, buying at unreasonably high prices, because that is what everyone else was doing.

Getting these deals was possible, because:

1—The original purchasers fell victim to the herd mentality. They saw unreasonably inflated real estate prices, and duped themselves into thinking that just because a very small segment of the population was buying, those prices reflected the feeling of the entire market. What actually happened is that most of the population did not buy homes during that period, but there was such media frenzy about rising prices, that the actual numbers of homebuyers got lost. And because of excitement and greed, those buyers chose to ignore the voluminous number of articles that warned about a housing bubble. They also fell victim to predatory lenders who were willing to lend to them on made-up income numbers, low teaser rates, and low fees. Borrowers were actually encouraged to invent and put on loan applications under a "no verification" policy.

2—I had money put away in whole life insurance. It was instantly accessible without asking anyone's permission or filling out forms (like I would have had to do to get a mortgage or an equity loan against my primary home), there was no penalty in accessing it (like there would be in an IRA), and I wouldn't have to sell stocks and bonds at a loss to get to my money (like an investment or retirement account).

In short, I hadn't followed the herd, and I had saved money for just such an occasion, in a smart way—keeping it accessible, while still having it grow nicely (unlike a savings account).

Chapter 3

HOW TO THINK SMARTER

Y OU DON'T NEED TO FIND all the answers on your own. Ideally, you want to learn from other people's mistakes.

The most expensive way to learn is to learn from your own mistakes.

The least reliable way to learn is from people trying to sell you something.

There are two reasons for this:

One: They may just be scamming you so they can sell you something that makes them money, and may not be the best for you. (You can generally spot these types of people fairly easily.)

Two: They may genuinely believe that they have the best product in the world, that it is the best for you, and that they own it because it is the best for them. These are the most dangerous people, because they are sincere, persuasive, and confident. To prevent myself from falling into this category, I run everything I recommend by a number of extremely skeptical people, so they can poke holes in it. I don't want to be fooled by my own misperceptions and prejudices, and I don't want to mislead my clients. I find people who are bright and cynical, and I ask them to challenge me.

Don't take what people tell you at face value—verify everything,

Don't let "experts" make your decisions for you. You have to live with the consequences. They don't. Hard as it may be, you'll have to become educated, proceed deliberately, and really understand what you are doing (and not doing) financially.

You will learn that the rules have changed from your parents' time. You are going to live longer than your parents and grandparents—maybe ten to thirty years longer. You want to be better off financially. So you'll need more money than they had.

Basic financial concepts haven't changed. You can still count on the same mathematical principles to work for you (or against you). But the speed of information has changed, and the way investments behave has changed as a result. Rumors spread faster, false information gets disseminated with malicious intent, and people unwittingly follow the herd, even if it is an illusionary herd.

The marketplace, and the financial product sales system, is rigged against you.

Every time you log into something, visit a website, respond to a message, purchase a product, answer a survey question, etc., you disclose information about your personality, the way you think, and your likes and dislikes. Marketers and advertisers learn about your emotional and psychological makeup, and target their messages accordingly. Their goal is to sell what they produce, irrespective of the benefit or harm to you.

No one who is successful tries to simply sell you a product anymore. They sell you a benefit. You don't buy a perfume. You buy the idea that if you smell a certain way, you'll be more attractive, you'll be more glamorous, you'll be more desirable, you'll exert a secret power over whomever you seek to attract, and you'll feel better about yourself. The truth is, you will still be the same person (and you ARE already attractive, glamorous, and a wonderful person, even if you don't fully believe it), but you'll smell differently. The same is true for financial products, and financial institutions. If you buy a product shown in an ad, you won't be living the lifestyle or feeling the feelings that the models in the ads pretend to have. You will still be you, but with a financial product that may or may not be best for you.

For instance, if you buy a term life insurance policy, there is only one particular brand, and one particular product, that is right for you. (The particular brand, and the particular product, is different for different people, but the way of identifying it is the same, and it always leads to just one product.) If you start shopping for term life insurance by looking at a brand, you are going about the process backwards. You should start by looking at the need, and arrive, much later, at a brand.

There are many good products available, and some are right for others but not for you, and a few that are right for you but not for others. Usually, there is only one that is the best for you. It all depends on you, and not the brand. It depends on your financial needs, and not on your emotional makeup. And it certainly doesn't depend on whether or not the insurance company is represented by an ox, a mountain, a lizard, a statue, a horse, or a duck. Or whether the company is ten years old or one hundred and ten years old.

But any marketer who is consistently successful with inferior products is using the system to take advantage of your weaknesses.

You also need to avoid being caught up in media hype and what "everybody" is saying. In this case, no one is selling you anything—you are hearing things, and panicking that you might be missing out on something. It is called the "herd" mentality, which literally means "following the herd," like cows, or like lemmings, who jump to their deaths together (at least according to Walt Disney). But it could also mean "heard," as in "I heard from someone who knows even less than I do, but talked themselves into it."

Take a look at Bitcoin. I don't know when you are reading this book, but as I am writing, Bitcoin has passed its crazy over-inflated phase, and settled back in an ordinary, normal over-inflated phase, which has ruined the finances of all the people who borrowed money on their credit cards to buy Bitcoin at twice the current price.

I fell prey twenty or more years ago to foreign exchange speculation, losing a lot of money in a field I did not understand fully, encouraged by traders who made money on my trades, (but lost nothing on my losses). They encouraged me to highly leverage my purchases on the assumption that an irrational market would continue to work in my favor. I abdicated rational decision making in favor of trusting people I was impressed by, and I failed to educate myself sufficiently. I fell prey to messages about myself (that I was giving myself) that were self-defeating.

By the time of the real estate bubble, nearly a decade later, I had learned enough to not be a sucker again, to wait it out, and to profit from the disaster that followed. I studied the market, and learned to ignore the herd.

Chapter 4

EDUCATED BUYERS BECOME
FINANCIAL GENIUSES

I T IS EASIER TO RELY on a salesperson's allegations and promises than to understand the policies you are buying yourself. This is a mistake for three reasons:

1) Most insurance salespeople do not understand the policies they are selling. You may not be aware of this, but I am, because I've met hundreds of them, sat in seminars and classes, seen the looks on their faces, and heard the questions they ask. If you are lucky enough to buy the right policy, you'll be fine. But it will just be a matter of luck. Unless you can explain to someone else how your policy works, it may not be right for you. It could be fine for someone else's needs, just not yours.

2) Chances are that the agent you are dealing with does not have a deep understanding of your needs, either because they are impatient, and want to make the sale quickly, or because they have not heard everything you said (like most of us in any conversation), or because you have not told them everything they need to know (because you forgot, purposely withheld information, or did not think it was important).

3) You have to live with the results, years down the road. Remember, you are not buying something that you will necessarily use tomorrow. Most likely, the benefit you get will be far into the future, when you and/or the agent are either old or dead. If the policies do not meet your needs because you did not understand them when you bought them, it will be way too late to fix them then.

There is more information available today, and it is easier to access, than there ever was in the past, because just about anyone can write anything, and have it repeated endlessly via social media. The proportion of misinformation to correct information is much higher than it ever has been.

This is because there are far fewer filters than ever before. Just think about it. A decade ago, if something was printed in a newspaper, or in a book, or in an encyclopedia, it was researched first, fact checked, and prepared by a professional. Today, anybody with a cell phone and a camera is a journalist, anyone can self-publish a book, and anyone can post an unedited entry on Wikipedia, or the like. Today, YOU need to be the editor who filters information to decide what is probably accurate and what is not. In order to do that, YOU need to be educated. If YOU don't understand, chances are that you will be taken advantage of. This may be of little consequence if you have been eating diet cookies for a few weeks before figuring out that you are not going to lose weight by eating that way. You just stop eating the cookies—no lasting harm done. The consequences are more severe if you buy insurance or other financial products. You will not see results from these products for many years. It they do not work right, there is no remedy.

Chapter 5

THE PSYCHOLOGY OF MONEY—
7 IRRATIONAL FEARS

EVERYONE SHOULD REVIEW THEIR LIFE insurance policies periodically, but few do. That is because they are possessed by one or more of the following seven irrational fears. It's a shame, because life insurance can be a huge waste of money if you are paying more than you have to for the product you get. You can easily overpay by $10,000 in your lifetime for the wrong term life insurance, and a bad decision on permanent life insurance (whole life, universal life, variable life, etc.) can easily cost you over $100,000 in unnecessary premiums in your lifetime. Plus, choosing the wrong product could deprive you of millions (yes, millions) in benefits that the right product would provide. (Just ask a doctor client of mine who would have lost $2,500,000 in payouts had he not switched.)

By recognizing your fears and realizing how irrational they are, you can easily save thousands of dollars. Do any of these reasons apply to you?

1—You are afraid that the agent offering to review your policies is just trying to get you to buy a different policy, so he/she can make a commission. This can be the original agent who sold you a policy, or a new agent.

This reason is accurate most of the time, because agents are generally paid a lot the first year, and little or nothing the following years, so there is a great incentive for them to churn you in and out of policies. Make sure you see the differences in the policies, in writing, and that they make sense to you and at least one other impartial, intelligent person. The sad fact is that half of the time it may make sense to change policies, because an agent sold you an inferior product the first time. (We'll discuss elsewhere how you can evaluate the motives, competence, reliability, and strengths of agents to avoid this.)

> 2—The first experience was so unpleasant that you never want to do it again, no matter how much money you will lose. Or you just decided you cannot trust any agents.

I hear this a lot. My sympathies. Do not do any more business with the agent who treated you so poorly. Find an agent who is more professional. Let him/her review your policies. If the policies are good for you, keep them, and have the new agent take over servicing them for you. He/she will not make any money doing this, but if he/she is a true professional, they will welcome a client who does not generate direct income for them, but might send referrals.

> 3—You still don't understand how your policies work, you've had them for a year, and you didn't like feeling ignorant when you bought them, so you are not about to put yourself in that position again. You were embarrassed to ask questions, and you were unsure of yourself, and you hate that, especially because you are very competent in your own field.

Right. But you have a responsibility to yourself to understand what you own. You could be spending too much, or walking away from a lot of money due to bad advice. Also, insurance is very complicated. Most agents are not very well educated. Ninety percent of agents drop out of the business in less than five years, because they can't make enough money to make it worthwhile.

This is because they remain uneducated, unethical, or just unable to communicate well. You deserve an agent who will take the time to explain your policies, or the policies he/she is proposing, so well that you can explain them to a spouse, friend, or anybody else. Find a good agent, even if you already own a policy. Again, a really good, professional agent will want to work with you and encourage you to keep any good policies you have, even if he/she will not be making any money on them.

> 4—You don't want to take up an agent's time, and then not buy anything. You are afraid they will complain to other people that you wasted their time, and that it will reflect negatively on you.

Good point. Bad agent. A good agent will not talk about you to anyone else without your permission. A good agent will also be capable of deciding if you are wasting his/her time or not. A good agent recognizes the value of talking to everyone (at least for a short time), and if he/she does not want to work with you, can gently explain why, and perhaps refer you to someone who might want to work with you. Everyone deserves fifteen minutes of fame in their lifetime and fifteen minutes of courtesy from every individual they meet. If any professional, not just an agent, is incapable of determining in fifteen minutes whether a professional relationship is worth pursuing, he/she is not a good professional.

> 5—You are afraid that merely initiating a conversation with an agent will lead him/her to think that you are granting permission for him/her to call you, email you, and stalk you incessantly.

Got it. Unfortunately, the way some of these agents have been trained, that is exactly what they think. One client of mine told me that he was considering getting a restraining order against one particular agent. I came out with a gag gift that people love—it looks like it says "repellant spray" and looks like an insect or bug repellant spray, but if you read the label closely, it actually says "insurance agent repellant spray." It's a fun gag to have—everyone wishes it really worked. Contact me, and I'll send you one.

> 6—You have a "personal" relationship with the agent and don't want to "offend/be rude/insult" him or her, or risk ruining the relationship.

Hey—I went to sales training school a number of times in the course of my life, but the most aggressive and offensive training I ever received was in the insurance industry. Properly trained sales people think they are SUPPOSED to make you feel obligated to buy from them. The others are just boors who really believe that they should make money off of you even if it is not in their your best interests. (There are also a small number of agents who have no clue as to what harm they are doing to clients, and genuinely, but mistakenly, think they have the best product for you.)

If someone is taking advantage of you, you do not have a "personal" relationship; you have an "abusive" relationship. If Aunt Rose insists that "to keep the family together" you need to buy from your cousin (her son), insist that she cut you a big check to pay for the policy, or write you into her will for the millions you might lose. Or just write the kid a check for $1,000 to make up what he will lose in commission, and hope she will pay you back. (She won't.)

> 7—You enjoy being taken advantage of by people you don't like.

Is that the real, underlying reason? If it is, there are masochism issues here that I can't address in a paragraph, or even just one book. But honestly, I get it. Modern society has trained us to expect people to try to take advantage of us, and corporate greed has encouraged people to believe that is okay. Decent people still retain a vestige of the mistaken notion that it is impolite to confront anyone directly, even when it is in self-defense.

Some of the nicest appearing, friendliest appearing, warmest sounding people I know are successful insurance agents. They were either born that way, or trained to be that way. That is why they are successful. But they put their needs before yours. That, for me, is a big problem. It makes me angry. Periodically, I blog about it.

PART II:

RETIREMENT

Chapter 6

THE FOUR TOP FINANCIAL ISSUES

One: How can you conduct your life so that you make more money than you spend (either by making more money or spending less)?

M Y FIRST FULL-LENGTH FINANCIAL BOOK addressed this. , It is called "The Financial Fitness Handbook." and is still available. It is great for people just starting out on their own, or for people who are having trouble making ends meet. It is also nearly two hundred pages long, and I am not going to attempt to condense it here.

If you have more money going out than is coming in, and you cannot figure out how to reverse the situation, read that book. Afterwards, read this book.

Two: How do you guarantee that your income continues if you are ill or injured and no longer able to earn a paycheck?

There are two ways to guarantee a continuing income without working. You can maintain a passive income (which is just another way of saying income from investments that you don't have to manage yourself), or you can have paycheck insurance, which guarantees you a paycheck if you are unable to earn money by working. Passive income usually comes from returns on money you invested, or that someone invested for you. For instance, if someone gave you money or died and left you money, and you invest it in stocks, real estate, business, collectibles, etc., and have someone manage it for you, you have passive income. If you have a trust fund that can pay you enough to replace your paycheck, you have passive income. If you can't work because of accident, illness, or disability, passive income would still come in. Most people don't have passive income, (at least in their early working life).

One of your goals should to acquire sufficient assets so you don't have to work.

In the meantime, you will be working to earn a paycheck. And an accident, illness, or disability that denies them a paycheck or reduces their paycheck (temporarily or permanently), can be devastating. Unless you are currently dealing with illness or injury, you most likely take your good health for granted. So far, you have been able to get up, go to work, and receive a paycheck at the end of the week. But for some people, life can throw them curve balls. During forty-five working years, people can become ill, have accidents, or deteriorate prematurely, and be unable to work for several years, or indefinitely. While it is not likely to happen to you, it can. And you probably know at least one person that it has happened to.

What might cause you to be out of work for longer than 3 months?
- Treatment for cancer, which causes weakness and fatigue
- Partial stroke, which takes months of rehab
- Major accident or injury, which causes months of rehab
- Sports accident
- Chronic pain that prevents you from sitting or standing comfortably
- Recovery from heart attack

- Stress due to finances, work, or domestic situation
- Severe automobile accident as a driver or passenger
- Severe damage from a vehicle as a pedestrian
- Onset of Parkinson's, ALS, MS, deteriorating back injury
- Carpal tunnel, severe sprain, rotator cuff

The point of this is not to scare you; none of this is LIKELY to happen. But unless you have a trust fund, or are well off, or have generous family and friends, or passive income from investments, life without a paycheck would be miserable. And if you become ill, or partially or totally disabled, and without money, it will be made worse. But there is a way to insure a constant paycheck under these conditions. I call it "paycheck insurance." The industry calls it disability insurance (or long-term disability insurance). If you work for a large company, you may think you have this already. But you most likely have short-term disability insurance (which pays benefits for up to ninety days in most cases). Or modified long-term disability insurance, which pays you only part of your paycheck, and under certain limited circumstances. Company-provided disability insurance is usually insufficient to cover your needs (and your HR staff may not know this). The income you would receive, should you become disabled, from a company paid for policy, is most likely taxable, which means that you will be getting 60% of your pre-disability BASE income (excluding bonuses), LESS income taxes, which is way less than you are used to living on. But you may not even have this inadequate level of protection.

The downside to disability insurance is that it can cost you between 1% and 4% of your annual salary. And chances are better than 50% that you will never get a penny in benefits. But if you do, it will provide you financial sustenance in a period when you need it the most.

So it's a mistake when you don't consider disability insurance. You should at least think it through. If you really can subsist without a paycheck, don't buy disability insurance. But if you need to get a regular paycheck, you need to think about what you are willing to pay to ensure that you will always have a means of supporting yourself. The pushback I hear from most people when they talk about disability insurance is that they're already covered at work. But it is amazing to see what is NOT covered in these policies. MOST people getting disability insurance coverage at work are underinsured and missing key benefits. MOST people with disability insurance at work should supplement that with a private policy of their own.

What would happen if you didn't have a paycheck one week? What would happen if this went on for several weeks in a row? What would happen if this went on indefinitely, for a few years, or more? It's a horrible thought to contemplate—your life, as you know it now, would change dramatically, and not for the better.

You can go from being "abled" to disabled VERY quickly—in seconds (in an accident), in minutes (in a disaster or natural catastrophe, or a sudden stroke or heart attack), or in weeks or months (with degenerative illnesses). Sometimes, the march toward disability is slow, like when arthritis or tremors slowly makes it harder to perform the tasks you do while working, until, one day, you just have to stop. But that is rare, as is total disability. Most accidents result in "partially disability," and it happens quickly. Disability has nothing to do with the type of work you do. Sure, some jobs are more dangerous than others, but most disabling events happen outside of work, or due to accident, illness, or disease. Savings can get eaten up quickly when there is no paycheck. Sometimes, savings are not liquid—they can be invested in a house, or a retirement fund. Cashing out may mean losing money, or losing your home. It can mean losing your retirement nest egg.

When I ask people about disability insurance, and they refuse to discuss it, I ask them to write a letter to their spouse, or child, and put it in an envelope that is marked "To be opened in the event that I am incapacitated." Then, write what you want your child or spouse to read while you are in a coma, in the hospital. Start by saying "Honey, I know you are glad that I am still alive after what I just went through. Unfortunately, we're poor now, because my paycheck will stop coming in next week. I never bothered to buy disability insurance because I never thought this would happen, and because..." and then fill in an excuse. I did this once with a lawyer who was making several hundred thousand dollars a year, and his wife took care of the four children, who were in private school. And get this—one of his clients had been sitting in a car at a stoplight, right in front of his office, just four months prior, and was badly injured when another car ran the light. And this lawyer handled the lawsuit!

Perhaps the best way to consider the case for buying disability insurance is to compare two similar jobs, and decide which one you would rather have.

Current job: Dream job, make $150,000 a year, full benefits, and you can work until you are ready to retire. But if you miss more than ninety days of work in a row, due to accident, illnesses, surgery, disease, disability, your paycheck stops.

Proposed job: Dream job, make $147,000 a year, full benefits, and you can work until you are ready to retire. But if you miss more than ninety days of work in a row, due to accident, illnesses, surgery, disease, disability, you still get a check, which is not counted as part of your taxable income, and is equal to your regular take-home pay. You continue to get it for as long as you cannot work (until normal retirement age), even if you get fired from your job.

Clearly, the proposed job is better, and getting that job is easy. It is your current job, with a disability insurance policy.

You might also want to consider how you would pay for health insurance if you were out of a job. If you weren't able to work because you were in the hospital or rehab or needed a lot of medical care for a number of months, you would want to make sure your health insurance premiums kept being paid, so medical costs wouldn't bankrupt you. If your paycheck stopped, would you lose the ability to pay health insurance? If you were out of work for too long, would your employer stop paying your health insurance? If the answer to either question is "yes," you need disability insurance.

The number of working people who are disabled for 90 days or more in their careers is higher than:

- the percentage of people who total their car once in their lifetimes
- the percentage of people who have a major fire, theft, or other loss to their home once in their lifetimes
- the percentage of people who are under 65 now who will die in the next twenty years.

Yet most people have:

- car insurance
- homeowners or renters insurance
- and some sort of term life insurance (either on their own or through work).

In other words, most of us have insurance on things that are less likely to happen, instead of on something we know is much more likely to occur. Loss of a paycheck for more than a few months would reduce most people to welfare status. The lost income could be several million dollars. (Note: Social Security provides disability benefits for working people. But it is limited, and hard to get. It takes time, there are denials of coverage, and, in many cases, the disability is deemed as not being eligible. And the amount received is generally less than your paycheck.) So unless you are independently wealthy and don't need a paycheck, you should have some disability insurance.

Here's what to look for when researching a policy and comparing plans:

- Guaranteed premiums: Get a policy where premiums are guaranteed not to go up until age 65. (Most policies will not cover you beyond age 65 or 70).
- Waiver of premium: If you are disabled, make sure no premiums are required after ninety days of disability, and you get back the premiums you paid in the previous ninety days.
- No offset for Social Security: If you do collect Social Security disability payments, make sure your private policy does not cut back what it pays you.
- Benefit period: Get a policy that covers you as long as possible (until retirement), with at most a ninety day waiting period for benefits to begin. (Shorter waiting periods are very expensive, and not worth it; longer ones can be a burden if you do become disabled.)
- Extended partial disability: Disability is not all or nothing—look for benefits that give you credit for being partially disabled. You are more likely to be partially disabled than totally disabled.
- Future insurability option: The right to increase your benefits WITHOUT having to qualify medically, based solely on an increase in your earned income.
- Retirement plan contributions: Are you participating in a retirement plan, or will you in the future? Make sure you consider buying a rider that will continue those contributions if you are disabled.
- Paying for disability insurance: If you pay the premium with after-tax dollars, your benefits are not subject to income tax. If your employer pays with before-tax dollars, your benefits are income taxable. Since most policies provide benefits equal to 60% of your salary, it makes sense to use after-tax dollars to pay for disability insurance, since the disability check you receive will be close to your take home pay.

- How are benefits computed? Make sure you understand this, and have your insurance agent show you where in the policy this is explained. Most likely, if you are totally disabled, you will receive the full amount of the benefit you signed up for, adjusted to your current income (because you purchased a future income rider, and you exercised it). Your income at the time of your disability will not be a factor. But if you are partially disabled, your income prior to becoming disabled will matter in determining your benefits.

- How should you buy paycheck insurance? You may have noticed that I mentioned, several times, speaking to your insurance agent. Disability insurance is something you want to buy from an agent in person, not through the mail, or on the Internet. It is too complex. Your agent should be able to work with you to get you the best possible coverage, at the best possible rate. Unlike life insurance, which is based on health and age, disability insurance also considers the type of work you do. The way you are classified affects your rates and benefits.

- Good websites to look at are www.protectyourpaycheck.org and www.lifehappens.org. One is hosted by LIFE, a non-profit organization funded by disability insurers, but it makes a good case for disability insurance, and has helpful details in calculating how much you need.

- Definition of disabled: Pay more for a policy that covers you if you cannot work in your own field (own occupation) if you are highly trained, and if you would return to work in a different occupation while you are partially disabled, and that work will pay significantly less than you are making now. For instance, if you are a trained surgeon and would make less as a practicing physician who did not practice surgery, or if you are a trial lawyer, and you would make less if you were not able to go to court, then you want "own occupation" coverage.

On the other hand, if you would be able to return to work and make similar money in a different field, while partially disabled, you may not want to spend money on an "own occupation" rider. It is more likely that you will be partially disabled than totally disabled, and more likely that you will be able to work at some job. If you end up being totally disabled, or presumptively totally disabled, then "own occupation" doesn't matter—you'll be getting full benefits. It is just if you are partially disabled that this provision would be important. (I know this may not be clear—please discuss this with your insurance advisor before buying disability insurance—it is complex.)

Three: How do you pay for your lifestyle when your working years end and you are in good health?

The key to not running out of money is to diversify your assets, so that everything is not invested in one place. This allows the various sources of income to increase and decrease in value at different times. It provides some liquidity so that you can take some money out without incurring a penalty, as you need it.

This strategy of diversifying assets is known as the "buckets of money" theory. It is very basic. Over your lifetime, you are going to amass various kinds of financial assets. You may have:

- annuities
- businesses
- stocks
- real estate
- cash
- gold and jewelry
- IRAs and retirement accounts
- collectibles
- bonds
- CDs
- inheritances
- cash value life insurance

- trusts
- primary and secondary homes
- other investments

These are your "buckets of money."

Very few of these are liquid at the same time:

- Real estate takes time to sell, and the market has to be right.
- Precious metals are easier to sell, but the market has to be right.
- CDs are easy to sell, but if you cash them in early, you can lose money.
- Annuities have withdrawal penalties for taking money out too soon.
- Insurance is generally a long-term affair.
- Stocks are easily converted to cash, but timing is everything.

The key is to have "defensive" buckets and "offensive" buckets.

Defensive buckets are the ones that are minimally fluctuating, easily convertible to cash, and don't have penalties to access early. Think cash, short-term bonds, cash value of life insurance, older annuities.

Offensive buckets are the ones that are going to grow, eventually, but that you may not be able to touch at certain times, such as when their value is down. Think stocks, real estate, investments, and gold.

The key is to balance your offensive and defensive investments so that you never have to dip into the wrong bucket at the wrong time.

It's that simple.

Keep it all balanced, and make sure that you always have enough in the buckets so you will not lose money if you need to convert to cash and draw funds out. Make sure you have funds in your defensive buckets that you can access to live on when your offensive buckets are low.

Never dip into the wrong bucket at the wrong time. You don't want to be selling stocks when they are down, to pull out funds for living expenses—you want your annuity payments to handle that. You don't want to be depleting buckets that you need to grow if you are short on cash—that is what the cash value of life insurance is for. You don't want to be selling investments that you are counting on to produce income.

If we group all the buckets listed above into four main categories, or larger buckets, the first three are the ones most people are familiar with when they think of retirement and financial security.

The first bucket is Social Security. Social Security is backed by the government, and despite the warnings of its imminent demise by so-called financial experts on television (who really have few credentials, and who strive for controversy and ratings, and whose main goal is to obtain viewers by scaring people), Social Security is solid. It will be there for you when you retire, in some form or another, as a secure base for your retirement income.

Another main bucket is your big, long-term investments—real estate, collectibles, businesses, and loans you've made to people. The value of this bucket will go up and down, depending on circumstances, and may even go to zero.

The third main bucket is your IRA, 401k, 403b, or other tax-deferred retirement account that is invested in stocks and bonds.

The fourth main bucket (that many people are unaware of, but which can be the most important bucket) is cash value life insurance.

Let's look at two buckets. (I'm ignoring social security for now, because you have little control over it, and it is supplemental, not primary, to your retirement picture.)

Assume that there is $100 in the IRA bucket, and $100 in the investment bucket, and you need $8 a year to live on (in addition to what you get from Social Security), so you intend to take $4 from each bucket. That is your retirement income—4% of these assets every year.

So let's say that your IRA grows 4% every year, or $4, and you take out $4 every year, leaving you with $100 in the bucket at the end of the year. If this goes on year after year, no problem! You'll always have between $100 and $104 in the bucket, and this bucket will never become empty. But let's say one year, the market was down 8%, leaving only $92 in the bucket, and you took out $4 to spend on your retirement. So you start the next year with $88. If something similar happens the following year (the market is down 8% a second year in a row, which is not unheard of), and you still take out $4 to live on, now you are down to $77 ($88 less the 8% decline, which is $81, less the $4 you took out.) By the end of the third year, you will need to get the $77 back up to $104, in order to be able to safely take out the $4 you need, and restore the bucket to the $100 you started with. In terms of percentages, to go from $76 to $104, the market needs to be up 35%! That's tough to do. A few bad years later, and if you keep dipping into the bucket, it will soon be empty.

If the same thing happens with your investment bucket, you are really in trouble.

The beauty is that everything is not in one bucket.

You may not always be able to take money out of real estate, businesses, or retirement accounts. When their value is down, leave them alone until the value is up. In the meantime, use the cash value in your whole life insurance. When you cannot go into your other investments because market conditions are not right, take money out of the cash value life insurance. When your other investments improve, stop taking money out of the insurance, and let the cash value rebuild itself.

Four: How do you pay for care if you need it in old age?

Most long-term care insurance policies (but not all) are simply this: you pay a certain amount of money every year to an insurer, and that gets you access to a pool of money which gets paid out, at a set rate, over a certain period of time, as long as you qualify.

The image I like to use is a blood transfusion: you buy a bag of blood, and it gets dripped into your veins at a prescribed rate. You can't speed it up beyond a maximum level, but you can let it drip more slowly, so the bag takes longer to empty.

If you don't use up the bag of blood, or the pool of money, or if you never start using it, you get nothing back. But the pool of money you can potentially access is many times the amount you put in, so basically, you are sharing the risk paying for long-term care with a large number of people, some of whom will come out ahead, and some of whom will not.

In order to get the money flowing:

- you need to be unable to do two of the six activities of daily living by yourself (eating, bathing, dressing, toileting, transferring, walking), or have major cognitive issues,
- a doctor needs to diagnose this, and
- you have to incur actual expenses—help for home care, or a payment to a facility.

The amount of money in the pool, and the rate at which it gets paid out, depends on the premium you are willing to pay annually.

You should only buy enough insurance to cover expenses that you wouldn't be able to pay for otherwise, from other funds. Cost of care today is usually from $50,000 to $100,000 per year, depending on a lot of factors.

Some questions you should ask yourself, when looking for coverage or evaluating policies you already own, are:

- What happens if you are disabled, or become disabled, or need some sort of extra care after retirement age, when you no longer have disability insurance coverage?
- Who pays for the care you need once medical insurance coverage no longer applies? (For instance, when ninety days pass after a hospitalization and your condition stabilizes, but you are still not able to care for yourself, and you are not getting better.)
- Who pays for care if you just gradually age, without any traumatic event, but just become increasingly fragile or unable to take care of yourself?
- Who pays for care if you become increasingly disoriented, and it is no longer safe for you to be left alone?

If you've planned properly, you will have retirement income coming in. This may be income from investments, retirement plans, pensions, and social security—any source of income that does not come from having to go to work. If you planned properly, you calculated what would be sufficient to support your anticipated retirement lifestyle. But most people do not factor in ill health, disability, or gradual deterioration into these expense calculations. All the advertisements you see for retirement funds show elegant upscale and physically fit retirees. They are dining by moonlight, or at a clubhouse, or walking leisurely on the beach, or playing shuffleboard or tennis, or visiting museums, or taking cruises. I have yet to see a retirement ad showing an otherwise healthy person in rehab after hip replacement or a fall, or being wheeled through a supermarket by a caretaker.

The ads never show a retiree getting off a wheelchair-carrying van to visit yet another doctor. But the fact is, even if you are still healthy and fully functional when you reach age 65, chances are about 66% for women and over 40% for men, that you will need some sort of long-term care for more than ninety days before you die. And there will be expenses associated with that care that are not part of your "healthy lifestyle" retirement budget. Aging poorly is a disability, just as an accident or illness is at a younger age.

Unlike your working years, when disability and health insurance will replace lost income and help with some additional expenses, disability in retirement is NOT funded by anything other than long-term care insurance, or some other source of income above and beyond what you budgeted for a healthy retirement. Medicare and health insurance will NOT pay for long-term care. If you have no means to pay for long-term care, your standard of living may suffer.

The quality of your life in your last years will be determined not so much by your health, but by how you planned to pay for your care if you are in poor health. The government chips in only when you become impoverished. Do you want poverty, and the government, dictating your care in your most frail years?

Aging poorly will cost more than you think. You will probably live longer than your parents. We conquered many of the major diseases that killed people young in the "old days." Today, if you live beyond your sixties, you have a good chance of living for a long while Most of the killer diseases that were killing people at the beginning of the last century are not going to kill you. The challenge is that you may have decades of slowly deteriorating health, and you may need expensive care.

The new "old age" is different than what old age looked like when you were a kid. It lasts longer, and it is more expensive.

What does this mean for you?

It means that you need to have a plan in place to fund the disabilities of old age.

Medicare does not provide long-term care.

Your resources in old age are going to be whatever Social Security provides, the assets you've accumulated, pensions and retirement funds (if you have any, and if they survive corporate upheavals), and insurance and annuities.

If you've budgeted only for your living expenses with these funds, it means you have not provided for the supplemental income you will need when you incur the additional expenses associated with being less able to care for yourself.

Relying on a spouse who is also aging, or on children who are raising children of their own, may not be a failsafe option.

Long-term care insurance is specifically designed to meet these additional expenses and needs.

You also need to think about where you will live in old age.

The choices are:

- in your home,
- in your child's/relative's home,
- in a retirement facility (either a group setting, or an individual apartment with communal dining),
- in an assisted living facility,

- in a skilled nursing facility,
- or in a nursing home.

Let's look at what these choices mean:

- Your home or a child/relative's home. Who is going to provide the care? Are family members going to be the primary caregivers, or will you need to hire outside help? Even if you assume that housing costs will be minimal, the expense of live-in or part-time help can be considerable, and Medicare does not cover it. And even with the best of relative caregivers, you need to factor in costs for respite care—your caregivers are going to need some time off. Don't make the mistake of relying on a spouse—if he or she is close to your age, he or she may not be up to the task. Or may be in need of care himself or herself.

- A facility adds housing costs to the mix. Plus, even in the best of facilities, many patients have private duty care to supplement services provided by the staff. This individual attention, even if just provided during waking hours, can run tens of thousands of dollars a year extra. But it provides a higher level of care, and may result in better outcomes for the patient.

In a nutshell: The less you can do for yourself, the more help you will need, and the more it will cost. The older you get, the greater the likelihood that your care needs will increase. The government will not provide this care unless you become impoverished and are eligible for Medicaid. If you want to hold onto your assets, or if you want to have sufficient funds to provide the type of care you would like to have, you should consider long-term care insurance.

There are several options for covering the costs of long-term care:

Option # 1: "Traditional" Long-Term Care Insurance (LTCI).

Although sometimes thought of as a new product, long-term care insurance has been around for several decades in various forms. It is only recently that there have been significant advancements in this type of insurance product, providing more versatility, and making it better suited to real life needs and conditions. Insurance companies are constantly coming out with new long-term care products.

If you have an existing policy it is appropriate to review it to see if they are still the best fit for your needs. Over time, your needs may have changed, so the policy you bought years ago may not adequately cover your current projected needs.

For instance, one client I spoke with about LTC insurance assured me that she did not need a policy—her mother had taken one out for her over a decade ago, so she was covered. When we looked at the policy (which had a very low annual premium that the mother continued to pay), we discovered that it would pay for care for up to two years, at a maximum of $50 a day, but only in a facility run by Christian Scientists. (I am not making this up—many people bought these types of polices.)

Since today's needs are minimally $150 a day, and an average of four years of care are needed between the onset of symptoms requiring care and death, this was clearly inadequate. Plus, there is only one facility in Florida run by Christian Scientists, and this client subscribes to a different religion, which is incompatible with Christian Science.

Similarly, some people have polices as part of their employment, at a low cost to them. But even a cursory look at these policies shows that the length of covered care and the maximum allowed reimbursement is wholly inadequate.

Another phenomenon in the marketplace is that insurance companies are leaving the long-term care market, as costs exceed expenses, which has made many older policies unprofitable for the issuers. One side effect of this has been increases in premiums for many customers, which come as a surprise to most, since they thought (erroneously) that premiums were fixed for life.

I need to strongly emphasize several key factors pertaining to existing policies, for those who have them. If this is repetitive, I apologize, but I'd rather overstate than understate these key points:

- DO NOT give up an existing policy unless you are ABSOLUTELY SURE you do not want it—you will not be able to replace it once you surrender it. If anyone advises you to cancel an existing policy, get a second opinion before you walk away from it. Let me repeat this to be absolutely clear. DO NOT GIVE UP EXISTING LONG-TERM CARE INSURANCE POLICIES UNTIL YOU ARE ABSOLUTELY SURE THAT YOU DO NOT WANT THEM ANYMORE— YOU CANNOT REINSTATE THEM LATER.
- The age of an existing policy does not automatically mean that it's either appropriate or inappropriate for you. A lot depends on the particular policy, your current and projected circumstances, and what other resources you have available.
- If you feel that you do not have enough coverage, sometimes it is advisable to supplement an existing policy with a newer policy offering additional features and benefits. Having two policies can be an appropriate way to balance the savings on premium in an older policy with the enhanced benefits of a new, additional policy.
- Because you were (much) younger when you bought your current policy, your premiums today are generally (much) lower than you would pay today for a new policy. Even if the coverage is not ideal, the benefits provided by an existing policy may be worth retaining. It might not be the type of policy you

would buy today as a starter policy, but even if some of the coverage seems unnecessary or insufficient, it may make sense in terms of total premium outlay. It is generally desirable to keep existing policies. Be very cautious before abandoning a policy that you have paid premiums into for a while.

Make sure that it is abundantly clear that you are better off starting anew before you cancel existing policies. However, if you find your existing policy lacking in coverage, you may want to consider adding a supplemental policy to cover the gaps, while keeping what you already have.

One word of caution about long-term care policies: Most policies obligate you to pay premiums for your lifetime, or until you start drawing benefits. While premiums are calculated so that they remain level from year to year, the companies have the right to raise premiums for everyone (not you alone) if they find that costs are exceeding revenues.

And that is exactly what has happened over the past few years—as more and more people took out long-term care polices, and some started collecting benefits, the insurance companies discovered that older policies were underpriced. So they went back and raised the annual rates, often substantially. This is bad news for people on fixed incomes. The policyholder's only recourse was to pay the higher rates, accept reduce benefits, or get back benefits equal to the premiums they paid in. While the insurance companies have raised their prices for new policies, there is no assurance that repricing won't happen again, either on older or newer policies. The only way to avoid a price increase is to buy a policy with a limited pay-in period, like a 10-year pay, or a pay until age 65 policy, and hope the rates won't go up before the ten years are up, or you reach age 65.

If you are looking at purchasing a new traditional style long-term care policy, you need to work with an agent who specializes in this. The benefits are constantly changing, the laws are constantly changing, and they are complicated.

Option # 2: Hybrids.

Hybrids are an option that guarantees a financial return on your premiums. More and more companies are introducing a hybrid permanent insurance, which builds cash value and has a death benefit, which lets you collect on most of the death benefit BEFORE you die, if you qualify for long-term care. The premiums for this insurance are going to be higher than traditional LTC premiums, but over time you may build cash value, and you are guaranteed a pay out when you die.

Of course, the death benefit is reduced by the amount you took prior to death, and the coverage for LTC under a hybrid plan may not be as high, or for as long a period, as a with a traditional LTC policy. A word of caution: Examine the provisions of these policies carefully. Sometimes the advertised benefits are greater than the actual benefits. At least one company promises that you can access 24% of your death benefit a year for long-term care. So if you have a $500,000 death benefit, you would think that you could get $120,000 per year for long-term care. In actuality, the amount they would pay is lower—it depends on your age when you access this benefit. This type of policy is designed for people who expect to need long-term care towards the end of their life, and has less money available if it turns out that it is needed in middle age or early in retirement. Nevertheless, it is a financially sound investment—you always get a death benefit, and even if you live to be over one hundred, the return on your premium will be decent.

Option # 3: High Cash Value Policy.

A third option is a high cash value policy, which involves a substantial, one-time initial premium. If you use it for long-term care, it will more than triple in value. If you don't use it, it will have a death benefit greater than the premium paid. And if you decide you want your money back at any time, you can surrender the policy and get 100% of your premium back. Your only cost is the loss of use over time of the money you paid. (These policies have a lot of variations, and allow for a lot of alternatives, such as using part for long-term care, and leaving a smaller death benefit—we can go over details if this appeals to you.) Buying a policy like this is like having a "free look" provision for twenty years or more—you can decide at any time that you don't want it, and get your money back. The only cost is what your money would have earned for you in another investment over that period of time.

Also, you can use traditional whole life, which builds cash value over time, to help pay for long-term care. After a decade or two, cash value really starts to build in these policies, so if you need to take out a policy loan later on, there are funds available. Of course, the amount available depends on the size of the policy, and you have to be careful to not withdraw so much money that the policy lapses.

Option #4: Bad Ideas.

Some people opt for bad choices. The primary bad choice I hear is: "My spouse will take care of me." This sounds well intentioned, but unless you are married to someone a generation younger than you, chances are that neither of you will be in a position to take good care of each other. Which means that your care will fall on your children, which is not a good idea for three reasons:

- They may not be able to take care of you—their life circumstances may not allow it. Chances are they will have enough trouble caring for their own children and planning their own retirement.
- They may not want to take care of you, no matter how well you raised them. Or their spouse may not want them to take care of you.

- It could ruin all your lives. It may disrupt their lives thoroughly, and lead to divorce, job loss, or worse, and you may not get the level of care you need. And if a family member (spouse or child) does take care of you, you have to remember that it will take a toll on them. Chances are that they did not plan on spending years of their life this way, and they are probably ill-equipped to staff all three shifts that caring for an invalid requires.

There was an article in the newspaper recently (I am not making this up) about a man who was arrested for housing his elderly mother in a shed in his garden. When the authorities found her, she was dehydrated and on the verge of death. She had been living in a room inside the house, but when he lost his job, he moved her out to make room for a rent-paying tenant.

Elder abuse is a problem. It was a huge problem when I moved to Florida in 1975, and I was part of a group that investigated elder abuse in homes and institutions, and brought about major reforms and regulations. I'm still reading stories about abuses by institutions and individuals, and legislators who are shocked, and promising to pass more laws. And 40 years from now, my children will be reading contemporary versions of the same stories. I won't. I'll be in a very pleasant retirement home that my long-term care insurance policy will be paying for.

Long-term care insurance can be a financial lifeline. This is one client's story:

Rachel was just short of her 63rd birthday, and her husband John had just turned 65 when they signed up for their long-term care policy in February 2012. They were in good health for their age, with some aches and pains, but nothing major or debilitating.

Their total premium was $6,400 a year, which was high, and only proved $150 a day in benefits for each of them. But it included 4 great benefits:

1—There was no limit on how long they could collect the $150 a day—it covered them for life.

2—The premium stayed the same every year.

3—The $150 per day benefit was just for the first year. It went up 3% a year. So if they had to start collecting benefits in a year, it would be $154.50 a day. In 2 years, $159.13 a day, in 3 years, $163.90 a day, etc.—and it would increase forever.

4—If one of them started collecting benefits, then neither of them would pay any more premiums, as long as that person continued to receive benefits. (In other words, it was free insurance, until one of them passed away, or in the unlikely case that he or she got so much better that they no longer needed care.)

In 2015, Rachel's health started to deteriorate, and by the end of the year, a number of surgeries made it difficult for her to care for herself. Getting ready to get out of the house was a slow, painful process, driving was impossible, and just taking care of herself was a huge task.

So she put in a claim for benefits, a nurse came to the house to check her out, and after ninety days (the waiting period she selected), the checks started coming in every month. Initially, it was $4,917 a month, and then a year later it went up to $5,064 a month, then to $5,216 a month the next year, and to $5,372 a month the following year.

And they were no longer paying premiums. In fact, the total premium they paid from the start of the policy until Rachel put in her claim was about $22,000, and so far, at the beginning of 2018, she has collected well over $200,00 tax free, and that number just keeps increasing. She uses the money for help in her home, bathing, dressing, getting around, and for someone to drive her around and watch over as she pursues a full range of activities using her walker or wheelchair. Without that help, she would be confined to home, and, probably, to her bed.

Chapter 7

RETIREMENT ACCOUNTS

Retirement accounts, such as a 401k and IRA are perhaps the least understood (and, if mismanaged, possibly a very dangerous) investment category

Background: A 401k plan is offered through your employer. You put in money to a retirement plan that your employer manages, up to a limit allowed by law. Whatever the amount you put in is subtracted from the amount you owe taxes on at the end of the year, so you pay less in taxes. Your employer may or may not contribute as well. Of course, the taxes catch up with you, because when you draw money out in retirement, everything you take out is taxed at whatever your income tax rate is at the time—what you put in, what your employer put in, and what the account earned from investments. An IRA is similar, expect it is just your money going in, and you have to manage it. The one exception is a Roth IRA and Roth 401k. In these types of retirement accounts, you do not get a tax break now, and, in return, you don't pay taxes on the earnings and the principal when you take money out.

These can be great investments, if you manage them well. But you have to manage them, and you have to manage the people you employ to manage them. Abdicating this responsibility is turning over the decision making on the money you are saving for retirement to people whose attitude to risk may be different from yours, whose skills may be less than yours, and who are trying to earn a living managing your money. This last factor is extremely important. How will these people behave when their interests in making the most money for themselves conflict with making the most money for you? (See the section on "suitability" versus "fiduciary" later on in this book.)

Here's why a 401k is good: Your employer will provide some level of matching funds, which is essentially free money that you wouldn't have received otherwise. Free money is always good. You will save on taxes now, and you will be able to put those savings to work so they compensate for all the negatives associated with 401k and IRAs.

Here are some of the disadvantages of a 401k:

You must eventually pay taxes on the money you put in, plus the money earned (if you indeed make money). You have no idea now what the tax rate will be at the time taxes are due in the future.

You have to make sure that the money you contribute now grows, and doesn't diminish, and that the growth is substantial in the long run. In short, you need to manage the account.

If you hire someone to manage it, they will charge you fees, so your funds will have to grow even more than if you manage them yourself, to compensate for the fees,

Good managers and advisors can be extremely worth the money spent. You just have to find them. With a 401k, you have no choice on who the managers are—your plan sponsor (your employer) chooses them, and there are numerous articles in financial publications about the extent of the problems in this area. With an IRA, the choice of managers is yours alone, but the challenges are the same—it is tricky to find and identify good advisors.

In a 401K or IRA, you can take out whatever you want, as long as you pay the taxes due, and the penalties, if you violate the rules. To preserve the principal, you shouldn't take money out in years when the value is down, because that can cause the value of the account to diminish to zero eventually. By law, you will have a penalty (10%) if you take money out too early, and a huge penalty (50%) if you don't take out when you are required to, in retirement.

Don't get me wrong—IRA's and 401k's are beneficial for most people as part of a retirement package, but not for all people. But they are not "set it and leave it" products. They have to be managed, and have to be just part of the retirement vehicle, and not the entirety of it. But that is not how the industry presents itself. The common message is "don't worry, we will take care of it for you," whether it be via advisors who will tell you what to do and make the trades, or pre-designed "packages" that have a "one-size-fits-all" model for everyone with the same retirement age.

And because we all would like to have things like this taken care of for us, because it is just one less thing we have to think about, it is easy to succumb to the temptation of finding someone who appears to be credible, and turn it over. But your retirement is too important for that, and the consequences of wrong decisions too severe. You are going to have to step outside of your comfort zone.

One type of retirement account is different from the others--the "Roth" 401k and Roth IRA retirement accounts. "Roth" is just an obscure name for a type of retirement account which you put money into AFTER you pay your currently due income taxes, and in exchange, the government lets you try to make the money grow inside that account without ever having to pay taxes on it, and without having to take the money out at a specified time. These can be great accounts to have, if you operate them in consideration of their limitations, which are:

- You give up the immediate tax offset that you would have received in a non-Roth account.
- You can only contribute a small amount every year, so you will need to save in other accounts as well
- You will generally only be able to contribute to your account while your income is below a certain level, so you may max out on what you can put in over time.
- You have to manage it to make it grow. It can lose money if you don't.
- There usually is a penalty if you withdraw money before retirement.

Still, with any 401k or IRA (Roth or otherwise) retirement account, all you will ever get out is what you put in, plus the growth, if any. The only products that behave similarly but offers more are cash life insurance policies, which we will discuss in depth later. These offer all the benefits of a Roth account, and all but one of the benefits of a regular retirement account, with:

- no limits on contributions,
- no penalties for early withdrawal,
- no need to manage the account (for certain policies),
- guaranteed growth,
- no income tax,
- and a huge inheritance for your heirs when you die.

Properly designed cash value life insurance policies are made to let you access the money, while you are alive (income tax-free), while you are alive (should you choose to do so), leaving the remaining balance to be paid out at your death. You can do this as a lump sum, a stream of income, or both, just like an IRA or 401k, but without paying taxes. We'll discuss this later.

Taxes on Retirement Accounts:

Pre-tax money, like what you put in IRA's and 401k's, is money that you do not pay taxes on now. In effect, you lower your current taxes, and you have more money in your pocket, from either paying less in taxes at year-end, or getting a larger return. You need to invest this money to make it grow. If you just spend it, you've lost the opportunity you were given. In short, if you don't pay taxes today, you'll have more money to invest, but you must invest it for the delay in paying taxes to make sense.

You will still have to pay taxes later, when your rates may be higher. So you have to make sure that you grow the money sufficiently in the interim to compensate for the taxes you will pay later. The taxes will be levied against both the money you put in originally, and the growth.

But if you forego the tax deduction now, and invest money that you have already paid taxes on in an instrument that is income-tax-free, like life insurance or a Roth account, you will not have to pay taxes in the future. And if you never pay taxes in the future, you'll have more money to keep and spend on yourself.

Chapter 8

WHAT YOUR RETIREMENT LOOKS LIKE, WITH 100% CERTAINTY

First, a definition of retirement: the period in your life where income comes in without you doing active work to receive it. Semi-retirement: You only spend some of your time working, and the rest of the income comes in passively.

Next, your objective: Have access to enough saved money that you can use, plus enough passive (and active, if you are semi-retired) income so that you can meet all your expenses without running out of money before you die.

Your death: You have no idea when it will happen. You want to plan to have enough money until the very last possible day, plus a week or two, just in case your calculations are off a bit. If you plan for an average lifespan, then you have to be prepared to live without enough money, along with half the people who are currently your age.

Your health in retirement:

1. You may be in great health until you die, and not need much, if any, end of life medical or custodial care. And you may have

the opportunity to do whatever you want every day. In this case, your only limitation would be your finances.

2. You may need some medical care, and/or help taking care of yourself to get through the day or get around. You will have some medical expenses, which will reduce the amount of money you have to pursue dreams, but your health limitations may limit how much you can actually do.

3. You may need a lot of care but have some ability to do what you want, or you may be totally dependent on others for everything. Your personal care and medical expenses would be huge—depending on the quality of care you want. This may cost more or less than what you budgeted for the healthy, active lifestyle you hoped for.

On top of this, you may have financial and/or time responsibilities for people other than yourself.

In short, you have limited control over your retirement. What you do have is control over how much money you will have access to in each scenario.

Income and assets in retirement:

100% certain:

- cash in the bank (invested in a cd, money market account, or just cash)
- social security income (depending on what you are entitled to)
- reimbursement for medical expenses covered by Medicare and government programs (if you are eligible and can afford the premiums)
- reimbursement for custodial care covered by long-term care insurance (if you have any long-term care insurance)

- income from any guaranteed sources (insured retirement accounts, guaranteed annuities, income from secure trusts, income from bonds, income from secured investments—just make sure you project reasonable returns)
- income from loans (advances) on properly designed cash value life insurance policies

The quality of your retirement depends on making sure that your planning guarantees that 100% of your "must have " needs can be paid for with your "100% certain income."

Your "want to" retirement activities will be funded by the leftover "100% certain income," plus all the rest of the income generate from other sources.

Make reasonable estimates of what expenses will look like for each of the three health scenarios above, counting inflation. Make sure the total of the "100% certain" income in the categories above equals or exceeds your "must have" income (which is the same as the highest category of expenses).

Feel free to invest anything that is left over at whatever level of risk you want. This will cover your "want to" expenses. If you don't wish to put any of your "want to" activities at risk, put more of your assets in the "100% certain" category to the extent to which you want to be sure that you can fund the most important "want to's."

Chapter 9

MANAGING YOUR RETIREMENT MONEY AND MINIMIZING TAXES

W HO IS GOING TO DO the best job of managing the money in your retirement account, and making it grow, and can you trust the government to supervise the people managing your retirement accounts?

Whoa! There are a lot of ways to respond to that, but the basic answer is yes, and no.

For instance, Social Security and Medicare: These will be around forever, in one form or another. There are so many people whose financial safety depends on these programs, that any attempt to eliminate them would get the entire Congress kicked out of office, immediately. As the number of retirees increases because retirees live longer, and the inability of their children to support them increases due to their own financial problems, those programs get more entrenched. They'll change slightly, but the programs will always be there.

Another example--retirement plan benefits: Yes, there will always be programs to put money away for retirement, either tax-deferred (like 401k's and IRA's) or income tax-free (like Roth accounts and life insurance retirement accounts). In the 1800s,there was no need for retirement programs, because you worked until retirement age, lived a few years, and died. Bu the 1900s, people were living longer, and companies starting introducing retirement plans. The devastation of the Great Depression spawned both government retirement assistance programs (like Social Security) and more corporate pension plans. But private pensions are, by and large, gone. Public sector and military retirement plans are still strong, but they affect a minority of the population.

So what's the problem with retirement plans?

There are two problems: taxes, and management.

Taxes: They are going to go up. As the government borrows more money, government debt and spending increases, and the funds need to come from somewhere. Whatever does not come from economic growth needs to come from taxes. So tax-deferred retirement funds present a challenge. How do you plan properly when you do not know how much you will have to give back to the government when you start taking benefits, and will the government change the amounts you have to take out, and the timing of the withdrawals, to suit their needs for revenues, as opposed to your need for conserving assets? (The answer is yes, and it won't be to your benefit.)

Management: Many retirement funds are poorly managed. They are either self-managed, which is another way of saying that they are not managed at all—the money just sits there, and the owners are too petrified to make any decisions, or the owners succumb to irrational fears, news stories, etc. Or people who are poorly supervised manage them. We already see a tremendous amount of attempted government regulation of these funds, which is an indication that there are problems with the way they are managed. But regulation will not solve the problem—the owners of the funds have to take interest in their governance.

Why robo-advisors are designed to fail:

> Every person's financial situation is unique to him or her. Robo advisors are designed to plug in information that ignores an individual's uniqueness. They are a fad, and they are not unbiased. Maybe they will work in the future. But I doubt it.

Here's how I imagine a horror story about robo-advisors playing out:

This is a tongue-in-cheek script of how a conversation with a robo-advisor might go. It is exaggerated on purpose, to make a point—the technology is not yet there. Think about how often you hang up in frustration when talking to a machine that cannot understand you.

> You: *"Hello, is this Swell Cargo financial advising?"*

> The robo-advisor: *"Hi, thank you for calling Swell Cargo's robo financial advising platform. I'm a machine, programmed by artificial intelligence. I sound just like a human being. I even have a name. My creators selected a name that sounds just like a human name you are familiar with, based on my guess as to your ethnicity, your gender, your age, and other factors. So please call me "Izzy," because I want to be on a first name basis for you. My full human like name is "Izzy Competent."*

> *"Yes, hello, um, Izzy."*

> *"Hi Louise. We've identified you with your phone number, and a secret voice detecting method, so we know who you are. But in case we made a mistake, please hang up if you are not Louisa. Are you Luis?"*

> *"Um, yes, I'm one of them, I think. You're close enough."*

"So how can I help you today, Larry? I'm programmed to understand all languages, and to answer complicated financial planning questions. I can even make trades in your account for you. I can help you make long-term plans for your retirement, without you ever having to speak to a human being. And I am smarter than a human being, even though one programmed me. So, Licorice, how can I help you today?"

"Um, could you speak a little louder? I'm 65 years old, and I'm getting near retirement, and I have trouble hearing. Please speak up a bit."

"Let me repeat that so we can be sure I heard you correctly. You want to buy 65 Bitcoin in your retirement account?"

"NO, NO, NO. I said I'm 65 years old and getting ready for retirement, and I need you to speak up a bit."

"Great, so I am confirming 65 Bitcoin in your retirement account. That is an excellent choice, Larry, even though Bitcoin is extremely risky, and really a gamble, and not an investment. But, you know, I'm just a machine, and you are the customer, so I'll do whatever you want."

"NO NO NO. Don't buy 65 Bitcoin—you'll deplete my account—I don't want Bitcoin. How can I stop this—how can I speak to a human? I need to get a human on the line—please."

"Okay, Lawrence, we will by some Humana shares as well. How many Humana shares would you like to buy? One thousand, two thousand, three thousand shares?"

"NO, NO, NO! Don't buy any Humana—nothing, buy nothing. I'm going to repeat this two times to be clear—two times. Don't buy Humana. Don't buy Humana."

"Great, Loser, we've just purchased two thousand Humana shares in your retirement account."

"Did you just call me Loser? My name is Louis. What's going on here? You 've just spent all my money, and put me in debt, and now you are making fun of me? I'm going to sue you."

"Sue, Sue? Hi, Sue. Thank you for calling Swell Cargo's robo financial advising platform. I'm a machine, programmed by artificial intelligence. I sound just a human being."

Click.

Why your 401k or IRA may not take care of you in retirement:

Taxes will dramatically eat away at your income in retirement.

You need to pay taxes on what you take out of your retirement accounts (except Roth accounts), when you take the money out. Your heirs have to pay on what they get when you die.

You are going to be taxed both on what you put in originally (for which you had received a deduction at that time), and the growth. If you do well in life, and retire in a high-income bracket, OUCH! Top tax brackets now hover around 40%. If they go up in the decades left before you retire, you'll pay a higher rate. (And it could be extremely high—in the U.S., we have had decades where the highest tax bracket was close to 90%!)

You cannot avoid the taxes by just not taking money in retirement. There are penalties for not taking required minimum distributions.

The year-to-year growth of your retirement fund will fluctuate, according to where the funds are invested, and how the markets do. Your basic expenses will probably be more predictable, and you will have little or no opportunity to cut back. Therefore, you may spend more in a year than you earn, and risk running out of money.

Remember, retirement is defined as the period in which you are not actively earning an income. You are depending on your assets and passive income to support you. If all your passive income is fixed (like in certificates of deposit), sure, you'll have a consistent income, but at current rates, you'll need a huge CD to generate any meaningful income, and most of us won't have that. If in any year you have to take out more than your investments earn, you'll risk running out of money. Expenses may rise, as you get older. Even if you had budgeted for increased travel and leisure that deteriorating health conditions no longer permit, you may have rising medical expenses and costs of care that cost more than you had budgeted for travel and leisure. You may also need to take care of dependents who are suddenly in need.

You have no idea how much money you will have when you retire, for two reasons:

First, you can project all you want about how much you'll put in every year, but your projections won't be exact, due to market fluctuations and costs you do not control.

Second, no matter how much money you put in, the total in any year might be more or less than the cumulative you've projected, even if you've earned a better than "average" rate of return. I'm not going to explain the laws of averages here, but counting on consumers to NOT understand them is how the industry gets away with publishing misleading numbers and encouraging you to make misleading conclusions. Don't take my word for it. Check out FINRA's (Financial Industry Regulatory Authority, also know as "the Government") Rules 2210 and 2211 (you can look for the details at FINRA.complinet.com).

Basically, it allows agents to present a thirty-plus page document full of numbers and charts, without having to point out that the least likely scenario is the most prominent chart, and the charts with the most likely outcome of the investment are buried all the way in the back, with an obscure title.

The basic fallacy of all these presentations is that they show a "hypothetical" rate of return. This means that the illustration assumes that each and every year, the exact same return will be generated by the market. This NEVER happens. (It also misleads you to believe you can average rates of returns over many years to get an "average rate of return." To provide a meaningful number, you need to also look at order of returns and volatility of returns.) I'm not going into detail here. Just enough to say that it is perfectly legal to provide irrelevant numbers, and let you draw wrong conclusions. Here's a good analogy: a travel agent sells you a vacation in Iceland, and tells you the "average" temperature in "Europe." Iceland is in Europe, but Iceland's average temperatures are lower than Europe's as a whole. The information is true, but not applicable to you.

In short, your best guess as to what money you will have is dangerously compromised by the misleading information available to you.

Once you start taking out money, it may not last as long as you projected.

Rates of return, velocity of returns, and order of returns will affect the value of your investments, and higher than expected living expenses may eat away at the total value you are relying on to generate income.

You may live longer than you had originally projected.

If you and a buddy together plan on an average life expectancy, and budget accordingly, one of you will die before that age, with money in the bank. The other will run out of money way before he/she dies.

You can't afford to budget for an *average* life expectancy. You need to budget by planning to live beyond 95% or 99% of your peers. Sure, you'll end up with money in the bank when you are dead, but that is better than not having any money in your final years.

The "solutions" some financial experts recommend are just silly and ineffectual.

Take one example, just published in an industry financial magazine. The "helpful" recommendations provided boil down to:

- Spend less in bad years (not so easy to do)
- Make sure your spending can be flexible (similar to the previous recommendation, and not so easy to do)
- Reduce volatility (which will result in earning less, and having to spend less)
- Use assets that aren't earning income (which means that you have to plan on having assets that won't earn income so you can deplete them in bad years). This is the same as saying you have to make the income producing assets work even harder. (Financial Advisor magazine-10-2-17)

The correct, guaranteed, solution? Don't rely just on 401k's and IRA's for retirement income.

Structure a retirement plan that has a solid core for the "must have" money to come from, such as whole life insurance, real estate, fixed income, etc. Use the less reliable variable investments, such as retirement accounts, for the "want to have" money, to the greatest extent you can.

Managing Risk in Retirement:

Let's say you are putting money into a retirement account, or a 401k or similar, and you add to it every year.

Let's say you have someone manage it for you, or your company manages it, or you don't pay any attention to it, or once a year, you look at it and move around some investments.

If you don't take wild risks, or trade foolishly, chances are it will grow over time. Maybe some years it will grow a lot, others barely at all, and even, in some years lose a little, or a lot. Over time, it will probably grow in excess of what you contribute.

When you retire, you stop the contributions and start taking money out. Now, the account needs to grow every year in excess of the money you take out. Otherwise, the value of the account will diminish, and you run the risk of depleting it before you die.

Let's say you planned on taking out 4% a year. This is not unreasonable if your account earns 4% or more a year in retirement. As long as you take out less than the growth the year before, you'll be fine— you'll never run out of money.

But what happens if in some years, the value of the account is down, and you still need to take money out?

For instance, if you start with $100, and the account decreases 8%, you are left with $92. But since you were counting on taking out $4 (4% of $100) every year in retirement, you still need to take out the $4, so now your account is down to $88.

So what needs to happen in the next year is for the account to grow 17%. That is possible, but not likely, coming off an 8% decline.

Maybe there is another decrease—perhaps 8% again, bringing the account down to $81. And you still need to take out $4 to live on, which brings the account down to $77. In order to stabilize the account at $104 for the next year, it now needs to grow 35% in one year, which is highly unlikely. A few more years of negative returns, and the account can be depleted.

This is what is known as "sequence of returns risk," and this risk needs to be managed.

You have four choices:

1. You can have contingency plans to reduce spending, so you don't need to take out $4 every year.
2. You can go back to work.
3. You can switch to riskier investments and hope for a better rate of return, crossing your fingers that the increased risk doesn't lead to even lower returns, which will wipe you out faster.
4. You can have other pools of money or sources of passive income that you can draw on in the years your retirement account is down.

Your goal is to build other sources of income, so that your retirement account can rebuild itself after the down years.

Chapter 10

WHY THE FEES AND COMMISSIONS ASSOCIATED WITH INVESTMENTS ARE IMPORTANT TO UNDERSTAND

THERE IS NOTHING WRONG WITH paying commissions and fees. You just need to make sure they are warranted, and that the outcome justifies the expense. You also need to understand exactly how much you are paying.

If you give someone $100 to invest, and he charges you a 1% fee/commission, it means $99 goes to work for you, and you have to earn $1 to just to break even.

If you give someone $100 to invest, and he charges you a 3% fee (or charges you half a percent and invests in products that have an internal fee of 2.5%), it means $97 goes to work for you, and you have to earn $3 just to break even.

Consequently the more you pay in fees, the better the performance has to be. So you need to see some pretty good indications that the high fee products produce really good returns.

If you open a tax-deferred (or any other) retirement account, and put $5,000 in it, and pay a 1% fee, you've paid out $50 in fees. If you add another $5,000 the next year, you'll pay $100 in that year (plus a little more because you'll pay 1% on the growth in the account as well), for at least $150 in total fees. Do the same thing the following year, and you've paid out a total of $300 in fees. Keep doing this for forty years, with a rough average return of 4%, and you will have paid out $63,161 in fees. Not even to mention that the money you take out after forty years will be income taxable.

If you buy a whole life insurance policy, and put in $5,000 a year for forty years, the commissions you will have paid (which are paid to the insurer directly, and not to the agent) will be about $5,750, depending on the insurer's pay scale. The money you take out will be income tax free. The cash you have will be dependent on your age and health when you took out the policy, and how well it performed.

Between the tax savings, the fee/commission savings, and the other variables, you could be way ahead with a life insurance policy.

You are always going to have some money in accounts that have management fees—there is no way to avoid this. And good managers are worth their fees. Life insurance will have lower fees than managed accounts, but it will produce lower returns (generally) than well-managed accounts. The challenge is to develop a reasonable balance.

Chapter 11

THE "BETTER THAN A 401K OR IRA RETIREMENT PLAN"—MORE BENEFITS AND NO RISK

EMPLOYEES NATURALLY GRAVITATE TOWARD 401k or IRA plans because those are usually the only plans they hear about.

And these plans can be great—especially if there is an employer match, which means free money. And free money is the best type of money you can get.

But after the match maximizes out, or if there is no free money (like many 401k's and all IRA's), you should look at adding other ways to save for retirement.

Consider this:

When you take money out of a 401k or IRA in retirement, you need to pay income tax, at whatever your income tax rate is in retirement, on everything you take out—the money you put in years ago, and the money you earned over time. (This is because you did not pay taxes on the money you put in from your income every year, so the government is playing catch up.)

- If you take money out too early, you will be taxed and penalized.
- If you don't take enough money out when you are required to, you'll be penalized—as much as 50%!
- If you don't manage the money in the account while you are working, it may not grow—it may even lose value.
- If you are successful in life, and are still making a lot of money, your taxes will be high.
- There is no guarantee as to what tax rates will be in general, but the way the government keeps borrowing money, it looks likes taxes can only go up.
- At age 70 ½, you have to take money out, even if you do not want to, and you have to pay income taxes on what you take out, and the government will tell you how much you have to take out, and how much in taxes you need to pay.

Also,

- There is a limit on what you can contribute every year, which is probably not enough to fund a long-term retirement.
- There are going to be annual fees to manage the money. Even if these fees are low, they add up. For instance, if you put $1,000 in an account in your first year working, and the annual fee is 1% ($10), after fifty years, you will have spent $500 to manage that $1,000. That means the manager really has to make your money grow a lot just to break even.
- If you die before you retire, all your spouse gets is whatever is in your retirement account. There is no life insurance component to provide extra money. And then your spouse has to pay income taxes on the distribution.
- If you die after you retire, all your spouse gets is whatever is leftover—the money you haven't used up yet. And as above, there is no life insurance component to provide extra money. And then your spouse still has to pay income taxes on the distribution.

So what is better than a 401k or IRA for retirement?

The clients I have who are successful use properly designed life insurance polices that give them unlimited access to their money, before they retire and after they retire:

- Income tax-free, forever
- Guaranteed to grow while you are working
- Never runs out
- No added management fees
- Pays out a lot more than what is in the account if you die while you are working
- Pays out a lot more than is in the account if you die while you are retired and are already taking cash out of the policy
- You can contribute an unlimited amount
- There are very few rules
- It is easy

So why don't more people use these policies? Because they pay very little in commissions to those who sell them (so most advisors don't even bother to learn about them), many advisors are simply unaware of them, and they have to be designed correctly in order to work properly. Plus, they do not have a "sexy" name with numerals in it—these policies are basically a well designed guaranteed investment inside a life insurance framework. But they have to be designed specifically for each client. An advisor must be willing to work hard to create a structure that pays the lowest possible commission to the advisor, so that they can put more of your money to work for you.

PART III:

LIFE INSURANCE

Chapter 12

HOW TO DEAL WITH
LIFE INSURANCE

- You don't understand insurance.
- Neither does your neighbor.
- It's not that hard to learn.
- If your teacher confuses you, you have the wrong teacher.
- If you can't clearly articulate why you own an insurance policy, or you haven't compared it to another similar policy, you probably shouldn't own it.

IF YOU ARE LIKE MOST people, you hate talking or thinking about life insurance. The top five reasons you hate it probably are:

1. You know you are going to be scammed and lied to. Insurance agents have the worst reputation for honestly and ethics, and for good reason. (I know. I became one because I couldn't stand how I was being treated by agents and companies.) There is a reason the industry is highly regulated—it needs to be. But like any regulation, the strict life insurance regulations, which mandate all the small print you see in policies and ads, doesn't weed out the bad apples—it just forces them to find other ways to operate. Don't take my word for it—read the financial news.

2. You are really good in your profession. You can hold your own in just about any conversation. Except life insurance and plasma physics. When talking to a rocket scientist, you are a bit in awe. These people are geniuses. And you feel okay being awed, because rocket science is complicated. And it is not your field. So it is fine that you do not easily understand it. But insurance is just numbers and risk and life expectancy. It is easy to grasp conceptually. You deal with math every day. But those damn agents make it confusing and they twist things around. And, frankly, they are not rocket scientists, so you are not in awe of their intellect. And you just HATE when someone who isn't a genius makes you feel stupid.

3. If you already bought life insurance, it probably wasn't a pleasant experience. In the end, you probably stopped trying to understand the product. You probably convinced yourself that you could believe the salesperson, because they were either a friend, or pleasant, or seemed knowledgeable, or seemed like a nice person who wouldn't cheat you, etc.) You certainly couldn't explain to someone else how the product works or why it was the best product on the market available to you at that time. In essence, you probably surrendered. Well, guess what? It doesn't have to be that way, and you shouldn't continue to work with someone who treats you that way.

4. The thought of going through the process again is nauseating. I don't blame you for thinking that way. But the fact is, life insurance is important. You have to get it right, or you will be wasting a lot of money, wasting a lot of money, or not accomplishing your goals for having life insurance in the first place. So suck it up, find someone who can demonstrate their competence, doesn't confuse you, explains things so you understand them, and compares products so you understand why one thing is better than something else.

5. People giving you financial advice probably don't understand life insurance very well. It is not their field. They know how to do your taxes, or plan your estate, or recommend financial investments. But they just don't understand life insurance, and they have no incentive to do so—it is not their field. So you probably feel unsupported. And you hate that.

Choosing life insurance is like deciding to rent or buy a home. Here's why:

Renting: If you decide to rent a home, you generally choose the least expensive home that meets all of your important criteria.

Buying: If you buy a home, you are looking for something that meets your living criteria, but also that makes the most financial sense in the long-term. Once you've settled on a property, then you need to find the best possible mortgage.

If you decide to buy, what criteria do you use to choose a mortgage and a mortgage lender?

Answer: You look for the lowest outlay of funds over time, so that when you sell, you've maximized your profit. The price you get when you sell your home will be the same, irrespective of who the mortgage company is. The key numbers are what you've paid out over time, and what the equity—the amount left over for you when the balance is paid off—is.

Why is this relevant to life insurance?

Renting: term insurance is "renting" a death benefit. When it is up, you have no equity, so buy the least expensive policy that has the coverage that you want. (See the sections on term insurance for details.)

Buying: permanent (cash value) life insurance is buying a death benefit, and the equity you build is the guaranteed cash value. You take out a mortgage (the premiums) so you can use the benefits, and at some point you own the policy with no more premiums due. In the meantime, you have equity that you can use (the "cash value," which you borrow out, just like you would take out a home equity loan.)

So what criteria do you use to choose an insurance policy and an insurance company? This answer is the same as the one regarding choosing a mortgage lender: choose the lowest outlay of funds over time, so that when you cash out, you've maximized your profit.

With term life insurance, there is only one way to cash out—you have to die.

With permanent life insurance, you usually partially cash out by accessing the equity in the policy at some point in your life (as an advance against the death benefit, either as a lump sum or as a stream of income), and your heirs get what is left over when you die. Of course, you can end up cashing out by dying before you've ever accessed the equity while you were alive, but this usually happens only when you die suddenly, and early.

Now that you understand the concept, how do you compare different policies?

Answer: For term policies, get an illustration of each policy, using the same hypothetical premiums. For permanent policies, get two illustrations of each policy, using the same hypothetical premiums. In one illustration, show the same amounts for cash out over an identical time period. In the other illustration, show the same lump sum cash out at the identical age).

Evaluating the results:

For term, choose the policy that pays you the highest death benefit for the identical premiums. Look at the death benefit for ten years from now, twenty years from now, thirty years from now, etc., and see which is better most of the time.

For permanent, chose the policy that gives you the highest total income plus death benefit, again looking at ten-year intervals, and see which is better most of the time.

If you are looking at converting a term policy to a permanent one, or cancelling a recently purchased permanent policy to buy a different one, ask for two illustrations to compare. For permanent policies, ask for two illustrations for each policy—one showing the maximum income for "x" number of years (such as ages 65 through 90), and another illustration just showing for a lump sum at some point in time (such as age 70).

Choose the one with the best income-plus-death benefit combined. Or ask me to compare them for you.

What is term insurance, and why would you buy it?

Let's say you buy a $500,000, twenty-year level term policy, and the best premium you qualify for is $500 a year. This policy will pay your heirs $500,000, income tax-free, if you die anytime during the next twenty years, whether that occurs tomorrow, or nineteen years and 364 days from now. And the premium will always be $500 a year. This is a great bargain if your sudden death sometime in the next twenty years would cause a financial hardship to your heirs. But that is extremely unlikely to occur (unless you are very old or extremely ill, in which case the premium would be much higher than $500. It would be more like $50,000 or $100,000, and most likely not make sense.)

Assuming that this is all you want, you should buy, (from an "A" rated carrier), the least expensive policy you qualify for. There is no point in paying more. If you live past twenty years, it will be worth nothing, and if you need cash before the twenty years are up, the policy will not provide you with anything. It is a simple contract: pay the premiums on time, and die within the "term" (in this case, twenty years), and somebody you designate collects the death benefit (in this case, $500,000), income tax-free. It is a great financial return, under the worst of all possible conditions—your death. That's why I call this "God forbid" or "death" insurance—in the unlikely and tragic scenario that you die within twenty years, your family gets some money.

Some term policies have an annually increasing premium. These are great for when you will only need the policy for a few years, and you are 100% certain that after those few years, you will not need or want the coverage. This situation rarely arises, but agents promoting the low premium in the early years sucker many people into these policies. For a few years, it makes sense, but after that, the annual increase in premium makes these bad financial products. Surprisingly, many agents are successful in selling these policies, often as "term to 80" policies. Their strategy is that they hope they that within a few years the dramatically rising premiums will serve as an impetus for you to convert your policy to a "permanent" policy, which carries a much higher premium and the promise of the possibility of access to cash while you are still alive. The problem is that these "sucker" term policies are only convertible to certain types of policies, which are invariably policies you would never voluntarily elect to buy in the first place, because they are expensive and inferior to most other options that you would have considered.

What most people fail to understand is how the conversion from term to permanent policies works, and it is too complicated to explain here. Just know that if you plan to convert a term policy, read about the details, in the policy specification form or the company-produced literature, which spells out the details.

Note of clarification: Some term policies may allow you to draw down on a portion of the death benefit if you are certified as being terminally ill, and about to die. This happens rarely, and it is one of two ways that you may get a payout on a term policy when you are alive. Also, nearly all term policies allow you to continue coverage after the initial term, at a dramatically higher premium. Usually, this only makes sense if you are diagnosed as having just a few more years to live. Again, this rarely happens, so, as a rule, do not expect a payout from a term policy unless you are unfortunate enough to die during the term.

Some term policies give you the right to convert to a variety of permanent policies for a number of years (at whatever rate is then in force for a person at your attained age) at the same health class as you were in originally. If you stay healthy, and nothing changes, this is immaterial—you don't need to convert from term to permanent, because you just go buy a permanent policy. But for many people, the passing of 10 or 19 years will affect their health, and insurance companies may assign you to a higher, more expensive risk class. But if your health does deteriorate, and you have the conversion option, they have to sell you a policy at a better rate than you would actually qualify for.

The catch is that your right to convert is limited to products offered by that company, which vary in quality, selection, and value from company to company. Unlike term insurance, permanent insurance has many features, benefits, and options that make some more desirable than others. The payout at death will also vary widely, even if two policies from two companies start out at the same initial death benefit. And the options and consequences of taking money out when you are alive also vary.

So if you intend to eventually switch to a permanent policy that has value while you are alive, you will definitely want get a term policy now with a company that has the product you want to buy later. You may pay a little bit more than you would with a company that offers you the least expensive term policy, but which does not have a good permanent policy. This is the only exception to buying anything but the least expensive term policy.

One last caveat:

There are two prices for term insurance: the quoted price, and the offered price. The quoted price is what you get when you shop online, or with an agent, or by mail. You give someone (or a machine} general details about your health, and an accurate weight, height, and age, and it spits back a rate. Then you fill out a form with more details when you actually apply, have a blood and urine test and let the insurance company check your medical records, and then you get an actual offer. And guess what? Those two numbers may be different. And the terminology they use to "rate" you may be different. One company may describe you as "standard," or "plus," or "super preferred," while another gives you a different label. When you go back to the list of quotes that you originally looked at, you may find that, based on the actual offer and actual risk class assigned to you, you no longer have the least expensive rate. For instance, if you had decided that you might be a "preferred" candidate, and applied to the lowest cost carrier based on that, you may discover that the carrier you selected thinks you are "standard" while another carrier agrees that you are "preferred." So the original low cost carrier may be more expensive. If you have only applied to one carrier, or did not let multiple carriers preview your medical records, before making a formal application, you may just accept the higher price because you think everyone will "rate" you similarly.

That is why you want to use a live, independent agent, and not the Internet.

Does it really matter if you pay slightly more than you should for a term insurance policy?

Does it really matter if you spend $1.50 or $2.00 for a bottle of cold water?

If you do it once a week, it comes out to a difference of $26 a year. Not huge, but I'd rather have the cheaper water and the $26.

If you are spending $500 a year on term insurance, when you could be spending $400, and you do it for thirty years, the difference is $3,000! That is a lot of money to throw away.

If you have ten identical proposals, each containing an identical product, but with different brand names on the letterhead, and a different price on each proposal, which one do you pick?

The most expensive, the least expensive, or the one in the middle?

I'd pick the least expensive. And save $3,000. Wouldn't you?

Then why do so many people overpay for term insurance?

Because they don't know any better, and the agent who sold them the insurance didn't care if they saved money or not, and maybe even made more money by selling the inferior product.

What is the easiest way to understand life insurance?

Life insurance is based on the knowledge that, in a given population, statisticians and actuaries know exactly how many people will die in a given year based on their age and health. They don't know who, but they do know how many. So let's say that we are looking at a population of 1,100 healthy males, age 25, and they know that exactly one of them will die in the coming year (that's not the actual number—I am making up these numbers to give an example). If each person puts one dollar in the kitty, there will be a pot of $1,100 dollars. If it costs the insurance company $100 to administer the fund, then whoever dies that year gets the remaining $1,000. Insurance is that simple. There will be a certain number of winners (or, more accurately, losers?) with heirs who have just received a sum of money, and it is predictable.

The older the group gets, or the less healthy it is, the greater the number of deaths and payouts, so, over time, everyone needs to contribute more money every year. And that is the underlying basis of life insurance.

You would expect that premiums would increase every year, because your mortality rate increases every year. But insurers found out that, for budgeting purposes, consumers did not like paying increasing premiums every year, so they figured out a plan. Let's say people wanted policies that would be good for twenty years. Since the early years would be inexpensive to fund, and the later ones more expensive, the companies just averaged the numbers, factored in something for investment earnings, and charged every member of the group the same premium for the next twenty years. (The same is true for policies that are good for thirty years.) In the early years, the pool would be over funded, and in the later years, the costs of the increased payouts due to higher death rates would be taken from that excess. At the end of the twenty years, the fund would be at zero, the company would have earned its fees every year, and the heirs of the people who died would have been paid. And everyone else? Nothing. The insured would get no money back, and when they died in subsequent years, their heirs would get nothing. And that is why their premiums would be so low—they went into the program knowing that they would all be supporting each other when a few of them died in the prime of life, when dependents needed money the most. Once that time period had passed, and the children had grown and the mortgage was paid off, there would no longer be a need for a big payout at death.

That's when insurance companies figured out the concept of whole life cash value insurance. What would happen, they asked, if instead of taking in just enough money to fund the deaths in the next twenty years, everyone put in a lot more money every year, and we invested it for them, and over time, there would be money to pay everyone at the time of death, and in the meantime, there would be a big pool of money that people could borrow against? And that is exactly what cash value whole life insurance is: high annual premiums, but a guaranteed death benefit no matter how long you may live, and cash value that you have access to if you want. Generally, it is designed so that the cash value builds every year, and that when you turn 100, the cash value is the same as the death benefit, so they just write you a check whether you are alive or dead.

Now you may be asking yourself, "Why do I need the insurance company to do that? Why can't I just put money aside every year, invest it wisely, and just pay myself a huge amount of money when I turn 100? And in the meantime, I'll have all that money in an investment where I can get it if I need it."

The answer is that you cannot do this by yourself. It takes a large pool of people to make this happen in order to have a death benefit. Sure, you can invest the money on your own, but you will not have the life insurance benefit. And because you do not have the same benefits an insurance company has—a long time horizon, expertise, and the discipline to stick to a plan, you will not do as well on your investments (unless you are very lucky). Also, investments you make on your own will be taxable; the proceeds you take from the life insurance company will be free from income tax. Sure, the returns will be conservative, but they will also be guaranteed. That is why you will end up putting some money in whole life insurance, and some in some riskier investments, like real estate, where the potential returns are higher. If you have a 401k or IRA, you will have that money (or most of it) in the stock market. And that will be the risky part of your portfolio, with the concurrent potential for higher returns.

Chapter 13

WHAT IS THE DIFFERENCE BETWEEN "DEATH" INSURANCE AND "LIFE" INSURANCE?

"DEATH" INSURANCE, COMMONLY REFERRED TO as term insurance, is designed to do two things, and two things only. One is to pay out a large sum of money to a beneficiary in the event you die within the "term" of the policy. It works like this:

- You get to select the number of years in the term. Example: you purchase a twenty-year term policy of $1,000,000 and agree to pay a premium of $300 a year (yes, it is very inexpensive). If you die between tomorrow and the next twenty years, (even if you die tomorrow, and only paid in $300 so far), your beneficiary gets $1,000,000, or whatever amount you signed up for. If you die twenty years and one day later, or after that, your beneficiary gets nothing, even if you paid the $300 a year for all twenty years.
- While you are alive, the policy has no cash value—you cannot borrow against it, surrender it and get money back, or anything like that. It is very inexpensive because it offers a very limited benefit, which almost no one ever collects on. Most people live

beyond the term, even if it is thirty years or more, and they often cancel the policy when it is evident that they are not dying soon.

The other purpose of term insurance is to insure your insurability— see below.

"Life" insurance has two purposes as well:

- a death benefit that does not expire (you always collect a death benefit, no matter how long you live),
- *plus* money (cash value) that you can use for whatever reason you want while you are alive

It is also called "whole life insurance." There are also hybrid policies, such as indexed life, variable life, universal life, etc., which do not have all the features of whole life. Some of these types of policies can be good; some are not.

The premium is a lot higher for whole life insurance than the premium for term insurance. The difference is invested by the insurance company and grows over time to provide the cash value that you can access. It is very similar to putting the money into any savings or investment plan, like a bank account, an IRA, or any other investment, with crucial differences. (Note: like everything else, you have to play by the rules, or you may not get the benefits. The rules are listed in the footnotes.)

The advantages of a whole life insurance policy are:

- You do not pay income tax on the investment gains. [1] (Subscripts refer to the footnotes below)
- Your heirs do not pay income tax on the death benefit. [2]
- Your estate does not pay estate tax on the death benefit. [3]
- The cash value produces consistent, reasonable growth. [4]

- The cash value does not need to be managed by you, and you do not have to make any decisions on how it is invested. [5]
- You can access the cash at any time by making a phone call and having the insurance company mail or wire you a check within a few days. [6]
- It allows you to build and transfer wealth tax-free. [7]
- There are no penalties or taxes for taking money out early (unlike an IRA or retirement account). There is not even a concept of "early"—whenever you take money out, it is the right time. [1]
- The amount of money you can contribute is not limited by the government (based on your income, unlike retirement accounts).
- You can use the money you take out for anything you want, (not just education, health care, long-term care, etc.) without disclosing it on any forms, just like if you took money out of a savings account.
- Your heirs get a lump sum death benefit, tax-free, when you die. This applies even if you die the day after the policy goes into effect; with a retirement account, they just get the balance in the account, less tax. [8]
- You can pay less than the full premium in any year, and still have a policy in force. You can even stop paying premiums altogether. [9]
- You will always have a cash value and death benefit, even if you stop paying premiums. [10]
- You will get more back than you put in, either while you are alive, or when you die, if you stick with the plan you set out with. [11]

The disadvantages of a whole life policy are:

- It takes a long time to build significant cash value. It is not designed to put in money today and take it out in a year, like a bank account. You need to think in terms of not taking money out for ten years, or more, depending on policy design.

- Whole life insurance is boring—you will never be surprised by spikes in value, or very high returns, and you will not be surprised by dips in value, or negative or low returns (unlike the stock market and real estate). You will just see consistent, but conservative returns. (4)
- You have to pay higher premiums, which will always be at least several times the premium for term insurance. Whole life insurance is an investment. Like any investment, you have to put money in for it to grow. It is a slow-growing, secure, boring, reasonable investment, that is a solid foundation for a retirement plan, and it is an insurance policy that pays a death benefit, whether you die tomorrow or in a hundred years.

Obviously, it is more desirable to have whole life insurance than term insurance, since with whole life you will get more money back than you put in, and with the term insurance, you will most likely never get any money back. The challenge is that you have to have more money available to invest in a whole life policy than you need for a term policy. So, if you really are limited on disposable income and have limited funds that you can invest in a whole life policy, you may have to postpone purchasing a whole life policy for a few years. Sure, it will cost you more in future years for the same amount of coverage (because you will be older and have fewer years of life left). But you have to remember that age is only one part of determining premium. The other factor is your risk class, based on your health, which will deteriorate as you age, and indications of medical conditions that you may start get in future years. So if you postpone buying whole life insurance, you will definitely pay an increased premium based on age, and possibly even more based on less than superb actual health conditions and projections. A term policy can be convertible to a whole life policy, priced for someone who is perfectly healthy at the age you convert, no matter what your actual health condition or projections. This is because the term policy has a right to convert at your original risk class. Let's say you are young, single, or married to someone who is working and can support your family if you unfortunately die prematurely, and you do not need the death benefit that term insurance provides. The only reason to buy a term policy, in this case, is to insure a low premium (and, indeed, to insure that you can even get insurance, in case of a horrid health problem) in later years—to make sure you can get a favorable rate, irrespective of health, when you decide to convert to whole. This can be worth a lot more than the small premiums you pay for term insurance.

Footnotes:

1. Provided you borrow out the cash value, or receive it as part of the death benefit. If you simply cash out the policy, or let it lapse, the gains will be taxable as ordinary income.
2. But they may pay estate tax if the estate owns the policy and the estate is taxable.
3. Provided it is in an irrevocable trust, or, if not, your estate is below the estate tax threshold.
4. If the policy is issued by an A-rated company, with a history of 75 years or more of consistent, stable growth and returns.
5. You don't "choose" funds or indices, like you do with some cash value policies. You participate in the overall return on the investments of the entire company, as determined by proprietary formulas that differ from company to company.
6. On large amounts, like over $25,000, you may have to fill out a form, or get a signature guarantee. But it is just paperwork—you don't need an approval from anyone.
7. If you structure it properly. If you don't, you could end up making it inadvertently taxable. Work with someone who knows how to do it right.
8. Except for suicide in the first two years, which may trigger the right of the insurance company to deny the claim, or outright fraud that would have resulted in them not issuing the policy in the first place, had they known the truth. Simple misstatements of fact, like a wrong age, or an undisclosed medical condition

that would have resulted in an offer at a higher rate, or a lower death benefit for the premiums you paid, would just result in a revised benefit amount to reflect what would have actually been offered.

9. After a while, dividends can be used to pay the premium in full. It slows the growth of the cash value, but requires less cash outlay. It may also reduce the death benefit. If there is sufficient cash value, you can borrow the money to pay the premium. It gets complicated and confusing, but if you want to "short pay" in any given year, look at several ways to engineer that and pick the one that is most reasonable for you.

10. It is called paid up insurance. The death benefit and cash value will continue to grow, but at very low rates. But you'll still have insurance.

11. Provided you pay premiums for enough years. The illustration you are given when you apply for the insurance will clearly show how many years it will take.

Chapter 14

HOW DO YOU KNOW IF YOU PURCHASED THE RIGHT CASH VALUE INSURANCE POLICY?

Too many intelligent, sophisticated people purchase insurance polices that are financially dangerous because they do not understand what they are purchasing. The negative consequences of their actions are enormous and sometimes irreversible.

One such type of policy is a cash value policy (whole life, universal life, or similar), which is sometimes bundled with a term policy, but can also be presented as a stand-alone product.

These policies are more often than not problematic because they will NOT perform as illustrated, but the agent glosses over this point, because it will kill the sale.

It is easy to figure out whether the policy you own or are considering is the best policy for you. All you need to do is:

- understand the illustrations you are shown, and compare them

- make sure you are comparing similar illustrations from different companies

By law, insurance agents are required to present accurate information. But:

- they do not have to present complete information,
- they do not have to present comparative information,
- they do not have to advise you that there may be other products that are better for you,
- and they do not have to fully understand the product they are selling you.

The reason most people end up with the wrong policy is because:

- the agent shows only one illustration,
- and the agent does not explain the illustration to make it 100% clear.

The key indicators that you might be getting the wrong type of policy are:

- you only see policies from one insurance company,
- you are unable to explain to someone else how the policy you saw works, in detail, after you have seen the presentation,
- you are urged to not shop between insurance companies,
- and you are not shown what actually happens when you take money out in retirement.

Strange as it may seem, the majority of policyholders have a policy that costs way too much for what they are getting, or they simply have the wrong type of policy.

For instance:

— someone who wants certainty may be shown a policy that has stock market risk associated with the premium charge, cash value, and death benefit. This is wrong for someone who wants firm future premiums, cash value, and death benefit. Often the illustrated premiums are low (but will not stay low, despite what the illustration shows—read the fine print).

— someone who wants a policy that has cash they can access in retirement is shown a policy that has disappearing cash values over time. This is wrong for someone who wants a policy that they can access while they are still alive

— someone who wants a policy that they can borrow against in the future while they are still alive is shown an illustration that does not show what happens when cash is taken out, because it is structured unfavorably for the client. The illustration they are shown (without the loan) looks impressive, but it does not compare well to other similar products.

How bad can the wrong policy be?

- if you have the wrong policy, and you go to take money out in the future, it may lapse, eliminate the death benefit, and cause you an income tax problem.
- your premiums may rise in the future.
- you could be spending money needlessly (and spending a lot!).

Let's take a look at a specific example:

A person who became a client of mine had purchased a whole life policy two years prior, from what we will call "Company D." He did it for the specific intent of having a death benefit in case he passed away prematurely, and a source of non-taxable retirement income in later years. Company D is one of the largest insurance companies, and it happens to have some good products (although not in this case). It is a company with a great reputation; but he missed the first warning sign—the agent's card just mentioned one company, and a little Googling would have alerted him that the company's agents (called captive agents) couldn't sell products from other companies except in unusual circumstances.

At 42 years of age, the client purchased an initial death benefit of $1,000,000, which would grow over time. The death benefit at that time was $1,012,254. He agreed to pay premiums of $26,081 a year for twenty-five years, for a total of $599,863. At the end of twenty-five years, he had a projected cash value of $1,014,607, and a death benefit of $1,790,000, which sounds nice.

But he did not ask what would happen if he borrowed money out of the policy.

I met the client when he was already two and a half years into the policy, and we requested an illustration showing current values and what the projected values would look like if we took money out down the road. We picked an arbitrary amount to borrow, $800,000, at age 68, and intended to not pay it back until he passed away, when the debt, plus interest, would be subtracted from the death benefit. He was shocked by the results.

The policy would expire at age 80 unless he started paying more premiums, which would be small at first and then become ever-increasing sums. If he lived until age 94, he would have to put in over $900,000 in additional premiums in order to keep a death benefit of $789,145, all because he borrowed out $800,000 at age 68. In other words, his initial twenty-five years of premiums plus premiums from ages 80 to 94 would have been over $1,500,000, and in return he would have received $800,000 at age 68, plus $789,145 at death at age 94, totaling $1,589,145, which is just a little more than he paid in!

So we looked at a different company (Company R), with a product similar in concept, but much different in design, and we ran an illustration starting with the same premiums of $26,081, for the same number of years. This bought us a higher death benefit ($1,116,886 versus $1,000,000) and a higher cash value at age 68 ($1,101,182 versus $1,014,607). The projected death benefit was also higher ($1,919,773 versus $1,790,000).

In this illustration, we also took out $800,000 at age 68. But unlike the original policy, the new policy would never require additional premiums, and there would be a substantial death benefit at age 94 ($1,705,905); when added to the $800,000, the total reached $2,505,905, with only $599,863 paid in. He would be ahead by over $1,900,000!

In a second illustration for each company, we looked at $25,000 a year coming out annually in retirement from age 68 on, and every year. Company R was far ahead of Company D in both death benefit and remaining cash value. At age 94, Company R showed $3,366,337, while Company D showed $1,764,786.

The net loss of a bad decision in this case would have been up to $1,900,000, for identical premium outlays.

I was able to get the client out of a two year-old policy and replace it, providing a long-term increased benefit, and by changing the design, save him $150,000 in premiums over the remaining years.

Chapter 15

HOW DO LIFE INSURANCE COMPANIES MAKE MONEY?

Simply put, insurance companies make money by using statistics and mathematics. They employ highly trained actuaries who are very good at assessing risk. They use accurate mortality tables. They know what they need to charge to make a profit. It really is a science. Out of every thousand people in a certain risk class and a certain age, they know exactly how many are going to die every year, and if they have enough people in each risk bracket. They just don't know who will die, and they don't care. (Only you care if you are the one unlucky individual.)

1. **Long-term investment horizons.** They invest in long-term, safe bonds, mortgages, real estate—anything safe, boring, and with a long-term horizon. And they keep enough cash on hand to pay out the claims they know will come in, so they don't have to cash out any investments prematurely (like you or I might have to do). They don't "play the market" like you might. Investments, not premiums, are what make them money. Premiums pay the expenses.

2. **Reinsurance.** They take out insurance in case their actuaries' estimations are off, or in case they have too great an exposure in

any single risk category. They don't make money on this, but it can stop them from losing money.

3. **"Lapsed" policies.** Some policyholders simply stop paying premiums and let the policies lapse. This is a great moneymaker, especially with level pay term insurance, where there are huge profits in the early years. Insurance companies love it when you cancel these early, and people do it all the time. They figure there are only a few years left in the term of the policy, and they are probably not going to die in the next few years, and the kids are out of college already, so they just stop paying.

4. **Growth.** If they keep increasing sales year to year, which the better companies do, they have even more money to invest, and their returns are better than projected. This happens a lot.

What happens to companies that don't make money?

They go out of business. But insurance is highly regulated by each state; the state is quick to jump in and take over companies that are in danger and sell them to companies that will honor the contracts. In the worst case, theoretically, payout will only be what was guaranteed, but that rarely, if ever, happens. Variable products that are unrealistically illustrated do not deliver what they illustrated. But the company is still there, making money, and rewarding the whole life policyholders.

People who have older policies can tell you that the name of the company they deal with has changed over fifty years, due to mergers, name changes, and state takeovers. But their policies are still good.

Chapter 16

EIGHT THINGS YOUR LIFE INSURANCE AGENT MAY NOT KNOW (OR BOTHER TO SHOW YOU)

1. Is there a guarantee, and is it sufficient for you? This is clearly stated in the verbiage and the illustration. Some policies have a guaranteed cash value, others just guarantee a death benefit and no cash value, and others do not guarantee the death benefit.

2. Are premiums level (the same every year), or do they go up over time?

3. Is it a hybrid policy, such as part term, part permanent, and is the way it changes over time clear? Does it make sense to get two different non-hybrids instead?

4. Does the structure of the policy make sense? For a term policy, is it for more than 30 years? (Not good.) Does the premium increase over time? (Rarely beneficial to you.) Are you on the hook for premium increases that are beyond your control? (Can't think of a good reason to sign up for this.)

5. At what point will you be able to breakeven? Is it worthwhile to you to lose money if you cancel the policy before then, just to get the coverage for the time being?

6. Is the projected hypothetical return realistic? Every agent can run projections at lower, more reasonable numbers. They usually don't, because the higher the number, the better it looks. Every variable policy will have a "mid-point" assumption. Look at that. The mid-point numbers are more realistic than the hypothetical ones. If the policy doesn't do what you want it to do using the mid-point numbers, it is probably not the right policy for you.

7. Are you being shown policies from just one company? Ask to see others. Are you being pushed towards one company? That's a bad sign. Look at the agent's card. Is the company whose name is on the illustration the same as the company on the card (often in small print on the back)? Watch out! The agent may be captive (i.e. unable to write another company's policies.) But more likely, the agent is better rewarded for selling you a policy with a particular brand on it, irrespective of whether or not it is the best for you.

8. Is the loan interest rate fixed or variable? What are these rates? Is the policy non-direct recognition (good) or direct recognition (bad)? Does the agent understand those terms? (Probably not, and that is a bad sign.)

PART IV:

CHOOSING THE
RIGHT FINANCIAL ADVISOR

Chapter 17

PROTECT YOURSELF

BY UNDERSTANDING WHAT IS MOTIVATING THE AGENT WHO IS TRYING TO SELL YOU A LIFE INSURANCE POLICY AND WHAT THE FEATURES OF THE POLICY ARE.

1. Any life insurance policy that either covers you at a level premium until you die (no matter how old you get), or that has a cash value, needs to be understood before you buy it in order to make sure it is going to do what you want it to do.

2. If you have purchased a bad or inappropriate policy, it is important to understand what your options are to reverse this potentially costly error.

NOTE: I AM GOING TO call the policies I discuss here "permanent" policies for the ease of communication, and these will include whole life, universal life, indexed life, term to permanent, and other cash value policies. My explanation does not include term policies. Term policies can either be level term, or increasing term. I am describing them below just so you are clear on what they are—I have another section of the book that tells you how to decide if term policies are for you, and how to best buy them.

There are 2 types of term policies:

1—Level term means that the premium is level for a certain number of years (usually 10, 20, or 30) and then you have the option of paying a ridiculously high premium that keeps increasing every year, or it expires worthless. This is designed to discourage you from using this type of policy as a permanent policy.

2—Increasing term or adjusting term means that the premium goes up every year (or every five years) until it gets ridiculously expensive. It is remarkably inexpensive in the first five to seven years, though, and makes sense to purchase if you are 100% sure that you won't need coverage after those few years are up. It also may allow you to convert to a permanent policy at some time, at your original health risk class, without having a medical exam. This is useful if your health deteriorates. However, the conversion privileges have limitations, and with most policies, you won't be happy with those limitations, especially as they pertain to what policies you can convert to, and with which carrier.

("Term to Perm," or blended term policies, are not really term policies, and are included as permanent policies in the following explanation.)

Permanent policies:

Underlying every permanent policy are three factors:
1. Mortality cost, which is what the insurance company needs to collect from everyone, every year, to make sure there is money to pay when you die. Every year, more of your same-age peers die, so they need to collect more premiums to cover the increased expense each year.
2. Expenses for operations, which are the costs of running the insurance company, including paying commissions.
3. Money for investments, which the insurance company collects to invest it on your behalf. The money is in excess of the actual expenses for operations and mortality. The income from these

investments goes partially to pay the ever-increasing mortality costs, without raising your premiums, and to build the cash value, which is what is accessible to you while you are alive. There are fees that are taken out of the investment proceeds before the proceeds are credited to your account.

The difference between one policy and another is mostly the expenses and fees and investment projections. Most companies use standard mortality costs.

Your non-cash value permanent policy is funded by the underlying investments. If they underperform, you may be asked to pay higher premiums or to reduce coverage. If you opted for a guaranteed policy, the insurer bears the risk of investment returns.

How your cash value, permanent life policy grows in value depends on the performance of exterior variables, like specific funds or direct investments. While there may be a guaranteed minimum return without guarantees, the policy can lapse if the investments do not perform well and you do not increase your premiums.

Accessing the cash value of your permanent life policy is best done by loans, to prevent the money you take from being taxable. If you borrow too much, and the underlying investments underperform, the policy could become worthless, and some of the money you took out could become taxable retroactively. You have no control over what will happen in the future, because of the variable nature of the underlying investments. So you could be hit with a tax bill decades down the road. With a whole life policy, you will be warned if you are taking out too much money upfront and are in danger of creating this problem. The numbers you are shown on what you can borrow are based on what the guaranteed rates of return will allow.

Chapter 18

ADVICE ON EVALUATING FINANCIAL PRODUCT ADVISORS (INCLUDING ME)

THE PRESSING QUESTION FOR ALL educated, articulate, successful, young, and not-so-young professionals who need advice is where to go for advice, and how to evaluate the advice they obtain.

For instance:

Where do you save for retirement? You know a poor decision will have terrible consequences decades from now, but that knowledge doesn't help you figure out what the right decision is.

What should you invest IRA money in? How much should you contribute to a 401k, IRA, or the like?

What types of insurance do you need or want (especially the kind that builds in value over time)? Pick the wrong ones, and they may be worthless. Make poor choices, and walk away from substantial sums of money in the future.

Buy, or rent your home?

What else can you invest in? Real estate? Collectibles? New ideas, such as Bitcoin? Start-ups? Your own businesses? Loans to others? Art? Precious metals and jewelry?

How do you decide how to evaluate advice on how much to save for your (future) children's college and your own retirement, and which is a greater priority?

Here is what you are up against in making good decisions:

1. Propaganda, advertising, entertainment, and targeted messages:

Let's be realistic. You have already broadcast so much information about yourself, the way you think, and the messages you respond to, that an advertiser can easily target messages to you that effectively address your trigger points. Advertising is an attempt to manipulate you, and the more you tell the world about what you respond to, the easier it is for someone to sell you something, be it good, bad, or benign. Sales pitches are craftily designed to appeal to your specific personality. TV financial advisors are actually just entertainers posing as advisors.

You know this. What you are unsure about is how to process it.

2. Pervasive lack of ethics:

The last few years have taught us:

- a—Truth does not matter. Say what you want, create your own truth, don't even bother to twist the facts—just state outright, self-serving lies with conviction. (Do I really have to give you a list of examples?)
- b—The government is not going to protect you. It simply does not know how. Plus, special, self-serving interests fund

lawmakers. Lawmakers don't represent you anymore—they look out for themselves, and their jobs. (Yes, some lawmakers are well intentioned. But, really, if there are so many scandals, indictments, etc., doesn't that say something about the group? This is not the cream of the crop.)

c—Businesses will do anything to sell you their products, including violating the law if they feel they can get away with it. (Look at all the fines, sanctions, lawsuits, and penalties that are reported daily in the business press.)

d—Really, really, really smart people, even some with great intentions, are being outsmarted by other people who may not be so smart but who are devious. News is fake, and financial markets are manipulated. (Check out the increased volatility of the stock market, the crazy plunges and crescendos, the insane Bitcoin fluctuations, and the like. What about foreign hacking and manipulation?)

3. Even well-meaning people get deceived, and you can end up being an innocent victim of someone who is sincere, but wrong, about what they know.

There is way too much information out there to process. Your expertise is limited, so you need to figure out whom to trust.

4. People in the business are constantly switching firms, and being paid huge amounts of money to do so. Where does that money come from?

These firms don't produce products—they manage your money. The money they make is from fees—it is money you used to own. Read the headlines about the billions of dollars being paid. Is this really because they make you so much money?

What motivates your life insurance agent?

Ultimately, you would like to think that the primary motivator of every insurance salesperson, broker, financial advisor, wealth manager, etc. is to be able to make a good living by giving the best advice possible to clients, helping them have the most amount of money possible.

And some sales people are like that. But most aren't. Most are just concerned with making the most amount of money for themselves.

How do I know this?

1. Anecdotally. In the past, I worked for two major life insurance brokerages. Most of the people there were new. I was told that 90% of the agents are gone within five years. They can't make it work, because either they realize that the products they are given to sell are inferior to ones that they have no access to, or they can't push hard enough to sell the inferior ones they are given. I would recommend doing a lot of research before you buy from someone with less than five years in the business. Of the ones who have been there more than five years, only a small portion sell in what I would describe as an ethical fashion.

2. From industry marketing. A substantial portion of the advertising I receive from carriers and brokerages stress the commission I will receive for selling the product as the main reason for me to sell the product. Obviously, this is a huge ethical issue, since you, the consumer, provide all the money received for the product. You are exchanging your money now for the promise of receiving the insurance company's money later, either in death, illness, or retirement. The more the company pays out now in the way of commissions, the less they have to invest in order to make the promised payouts to you later. So if they pay out a lot in commissions, they have to do a heck of a job investing the

money—better than their competitors. It is just not going to happen.

3. From government regulators. The industry is really in an uproar now, because the government (the Department of Labor) has tried to pass a regulation mandating "fiduciary advice" over "suitable advice" on some products in some types of accounts. It's been all-consuming for the industry, and has forced a lot of changes in the way many advisors run their businesses, but the underlying message to the layperson is simple. "Suitable" means exactly what it sounds like—"it's okay." It's not the best, and it's not the worst; it's just okay. If someone sends you to the store to buy a white dress shirt and gives you $100 to do it, and you pick up the first one you see in the correct size, and it costs just about $100, you acted suitably. But if you searched for something on sale, compared fabric quality, looked for the best fit in the right size, used coupons that you researched, got rewards points that you put on the buyer's account (and not yours), you acted as a fiduciary. The government recognizes that without regulation, advisors will most likely use a suitability standard, to the detriment of their clients. Unfortunately, the industry pushes back against the adoption of mandatory fiduciary standards, and consumers are not clear on what is motivating the advisors.

Who is looking out for you?

You may have missed all the "news" in the financial industry recently, especially if you are not on the incessant "news" feeds. But you really should be paying attention, because it is important to your financial future.

Basically, what has happened is that the U.S. Government (Department of Labor) has "suddenly" woken up and realized with a shock that some financial advisors might have conflicts of interest when recommending products to their clients. So they are seeking to impose stricter standards, requiring advisors to act solely in the best interests of their clients, and to disclose conflicts, and fees!

Surprise—you would have thought that by regulating advisors and registering them, the minimal standard would have already been the client's best interests, but it's not--most investments just have to be "suitable."

That doesn't sound like this is a very good arrangement for you, and I've been saying that for years. You have to know who you are taking advice from, what their qualifications are, how they are compensated, what their conflicts are, and why they are only showing you the options they choose to present. Nearly all the advisors in the business have access to just a limited range of products, and very few will encourage you to go and explore the products they don't handle.

In other words, suitable is just okay, and fiduciary is in your best interest.

So why is the industry so upset that it is being required to act as a fiduciary for clients in only one type of account for some types of products? Because it means they can't sell you what they've been selling you, where they make the biggest commissions, and where they benefit the most, while giving you something "just okay." But the real horror story is that the rule only applies to a small group of products in specific situations. That means, for everything else, it is business as usual, selling you something that is merely suitable, and that may be a better deal for the salesperson than the customer! And here you were, all along, thinking that this person who cold-called you, or was recommended by a friend, or who chatted you up at a meeting or a party, had your best interests at heart!

Note: As this book goes to press, the government has backed down from the fiduciary standard on the limited number of products they tried to impose it on. So it is back to "caveat emptor."

So where do you go for advice, and how do you evaluate the advice you get?

- You go to someone who can explain what he or she is recommending, so that you fully understand it. Hearing "trust me" from someone who has not explained something clearly should be a conversation ender for you.

- You go to someone who will listen to you.

- You go to someone who can show you numbers that seem reasonable and that you can understand.

- You go to someone who is independent.

- You go to someone you respect, who has been in your shoes, and who is respected by the community.

- You go to someone who withstands rigorous scrutiny.

- You go to someone you can trust in helping you make life's most importance decisions for you. Because, ultimately, that may be what you are doing.

Chapter 19

A FOOLPROOF WAY TO CHOOSE A FINANCIAL ADVISOR

FINANCIAL ADVISORS CANNOT OFFER YOU market guarantees.

Financial advisors cannot replicate past performances.

Financial advisors may have limited access to investment options, depending on their license status and what their firms permit them to sell—no one has access, or knowledge of, everything available.

So you cannot choose a financial advisor based on past performance or anticipated investment results. You can scrutinize them more closely based on whom they chose to work for.

What you want to ascertain is how they think, how they use resources, and how they learn over time.

Start by doing the following:

1. Go online and look up the advisor on FINRA. It is a government website that reports employment history, licensing status, and

disciplinary actions. It is not complete and sometimes omits important history, but it's a start.

2. Scour social media and the search engines for news and reviews. Check out both the person and the company. Pay special attention to the company. How tightly do they control what an advisor can do? How hard do they push products designed to benefit their company, or the product manufacturer, as opposed to providing the best value for you?

3. Ask for references from people you know. The goal is not to see what those clients did, or what the outcome was, but to assess how the advisor runs his/her business. Are calls returned promptly? Are they available to meet? Do they provide ongoing updates to clients without being prompted? In other words, will you get the service you need? Don't ask them about performance. Most clients are clueless as to how their portfolio is performing.

This will give you a good idea if you want to keep this advisor in consideration. If you do, then:

4. Ask what they recommended or placed for their last five clients, and why they thought it was right. Are they really paying attention to varying needs, or are they selling the same products to everyone? Why?

5. Ask about life insurance and disability policies that they personally own, and why they chose those products. This may be the most important information you get, because:

   a. You can always change financial advisors, firms, or products. The values go up and down, and you can easily take a profit, or a loss, and move on. Portfolios can recover. But insurance should be a permanent product. You need to make the right choice the first time. After a few years, it becomes expensive, if not impossible, to make changes, both because of your older age, and possibly, worse health. Bad choices made early on just get worse over time.

b. Financial advisors are notoriously unfamiliar with life and disability insurance. They usually buy insurance based on what they are promised or told, and not what they have researched.

c. If advisors are part of a large firm, they are encouraged to refer you to specialists within the firm, who are limited with what they can sell by firm agreements. This is not a good sign as to an advisor's ability to think independently and evaluate his/her own finances.

d. If you purchase from someone who is "captive" (required to sell only products produced by their firm) or even someone who affiliates with a particular insurance company, your advisor may not have done sufficient research to recommend you to a product that he or she does not handle, because there is no incentive to do so.

What to Look for in a Financial Advisor:

There are nine qualities to look for in a financial advisor, but there is one word that sums them all up, and that word is "humility." Humility means being upfront in telling you that they do not know everything, and that they will not have solutions until they get to know you, your situation, your needs, and have a chance to research the issues, and consult with others. When you ask questions of a potential advisor, the response you are looking for, more than half the time, is, "I don't know; let me find out and get back to you." Then, when they do get back to you, more than half the time, when you have follow up questions, the answer you are looking for is, "I don't know; let me find out and get back to you."

If, instead, you always hear immediate responses, you are dealing with a salesperson, and not an advisor. The difference is that a salesperson has been trained to listen for certain words, and spit out a canned answer.

QUALITY #1: The ability to listen.

Your situation is unique. Describe it to your advisor. Tell him or her what your needs are. Know your goals. Can he or she repeat them back to you, without notes? If not, find a different advisor—this one isn't listening.

QUALITY #2: The ability to communicate clearly.

Repeat back your understanding of what you are being told. Make your advisor explain the abbreviations to you. Make sure you understand what they stand for, and how those concepts apply to you. Something that sounds too good to be true usually is—remember, highly sophisticated people fell for Ponzi schemes and the collateralized debt obligations (CDO's) that sunk Lehman Brothers and major banks. Most people who sold CDO's did not understand them. Read any of the books about the collapse of 2008, most notably Barry Dyke's "The Pirates of Manhattan," to see just how frighteningly ignorant the greedy and overpaid salespeople/con artists who ran major funds and banks were. They did not know about what they were buying and selling. Don't stop there—go back and read about the tulip bulb craze of the 1620's in Holland. Put the two together, and you'll see that in 400 years, nothing has changed: clever people who are willing to take advantage of others can always find someone gullible.

QUALITY #3: The ability to see you as an individual.

Your financial situation and your goals are unique to you. How customized is the proposed solution that is presented to you? How well does each piece address your needs?

QUALITY #4: Competency and intelligence.

Check references. Who does the person work with? What is his or her reputation? What are his or her strengths? What do all the letters after his or her name mean? Google each one—if he or she is boasting credentials that require just membership in an organization, and no experience or qualifying education, be suspicious.

Mary L. Shapiro, the CEO of FINRA—a government group responsible for regulating the financial industry—said on 9/10/2007 about a pending regulatory action: "The first sweep is aimed at the use of inflated or meaningless titles by advisers who are seeking to lure seniors into thinking they are experts in retirement planning. The use of so-called professional designations is becoming an increasingly common device used to open an account. The unfortunate truth is that seniors can be susceptible to these tactics. Our research shows that some seniors are more likely to listen to pitches from people with such designations… The unfortunate fact is that some designations can be obtained by simply paying membership dues to an organization with an impressive sounding name. Too many times these designations mean absolutely nothing. Seniors put their trust in these individuals and are led down a path of financial ruin."

QUALITY #5: Connectivity.

Who does your advisor go to for advice? No advisor can know everything—the key is knowing where to go to learn what is right for you. Who are your advisor's advisors?

If your advisor cannot call on a wide range of experts to fashion a solution for you, it means he or she is regularly selling a small set of products that he or she knows well, and is not open to spending time to learn what is best for you. Can he or she run through a "what if" scenario with you? Provide reasonable projections of your financial trajectory? Summarize recommendations clearly? Or is it a hodge-podge?

QUALITY #6: Concern.

This is my biggest area of annoyance. Too many advisors are sales motivated—find the client, present a product, make the sale, collect the commission, move on. You need to flip it around. It's your money, and your future. The commission payout of most products is huge. Your advisor has to be looking at your situation from your perspective. He or she is being well compensated. There is only one chance to get it right. You'll never have a chance to go back thirty years and begin your earning experience over again. If an advisor implies that you are taking up too much time, or asking too many questions, or looking for too many quotes, then it's not the right fit for either of you. Leave.

QUALITY #7: Compatibility.

Unless you share similar values, it's hard for your advisor to get on your wavelength. I'm not talking about sharing hobbies, or even community involvement. What I am speaking about is the values that lead to hobbies and community involvement—priorities, ethics, and the role each of you play in the community. You are talking about plans that will shape your life and your children's lives. Don't you want to do this with someone who has the same values as you?

QUALITY #8: Confidentiality.

Are you being told things about other clients that you would not want other people to know about you? If so, leave. When you go to your advisor's office, are other client files readily visible? When you view files on your advisor's computer, do you end up glimpsing information about other clients? Are your advisor's files labeled with client names, or is each client assigned a discreet number? (I limit the use of names on physical and computer files so that there is maximum privacy. And I don't tell clients or potential clients the names of other clients, unless I have specific permission to do so.)

QUALITY #9: Follow through.

Does your advisor follow through when promised, in a reasonable timeframe? Don't expect immediate answers—developing recommendations can take time, and you are one of several clients. But your advisor needs to be able to acknowledge your inquiries, respect your time horizons, and follow through on delivering information when promised. If he or she doesn't, leave. That person is either too busy for you, or you are not important enough to him or her.

Either way, it's a bad fit for you.

PART V:

GENERAL MONEY ADVICE

Chapter 20

THE TOP MONEY QUESTIONS

T̲HERE ARE SOME QUESTIONS I hear more frequently than others. I've grouped them together here, in no particular order, for convenience.

Student loans: should you get them, and if you get them, when and how should you pay them off?

If you are reading this book, chances are that you have already started, or more likely completed, your higher education. In which case, the question of whether or not to get student loans is moot. How to pay them off is now the issue. The answer involves the use of a spreadsheet, because it is a mathematical one. Since one of your goals in life probably is the accumulation of usable money, the real question is not whether or not you should pay loans off quickly, but rather how you evaluate the benefits of other options that you have.

There are two types of money: accumulated money and usable money. Accumulated money is money in the bank, money in investments, money in reserves or trusts, money that you will be able to use in the future (but not now), money that is working for you to create income or more money, but which has no immediate benefit to you. For instance, a retirement account is accumulated money. You derive no benefit from it now, except for the comfort of knowing that you will have usable money later. Gold is accumulated money. Unless you fashion it into jewelry, it has no immediate use, except, as with all accumulated money, peace of mind that it will become usable later. Anticipated inheritances are another example of accumulated money. Etcetera.

Usable money is cash you can immediately spend. (Checking accounts, cash in your wallet, your paycheck, etc.)

In some cases, there is hybrid money—accumulated money that produces usable money or an immediate benefit. Consider art or collectibles, for instance—you enjoy looking at them while they grow in value. Your home—you enjoy living in it while it grows in value. Buying a warehouse for your business—you save on rent, and it grows in value.

So the question of paying off student loans is, really, what is the benefit of being debt-free, and what else could you do with the money? For instance, you may get a tax break on student loan interest. If you pay off the loan, you lose the tax break. So what can you do with the tax refund that makes it produce more money than you would be saving by not paying the student loan interest? (Probably not a lot, unless you are using it to pay off high-interest credit card debt.) What are the opportunity costs of not converting the money you would have used to pay the loan (usable money) to accumulated money? If you purchased something solid that would really grow over time, like a cash value life insurance policy, would the net benefit, in retirement, be better than immediate disadvantage of a reduced loan and lower interest payments? Would it outweigh the "peace of mind" that you envision from being debt-free? Or is that "peace of mind" illusionary, because you are ignoring the "unsettling restlessness of mind" that can accompany debt? Spoiler alert! There is no one single correct answer to this question.

What are the best retirement funds, and why?

This is a trick question.

The reason that it is a trick question is because any place you put your money now, to grow so you can use it later, is, by implication, a "retirement fund." Even if you are collecting uncirculated baseball cards, it is a retirement fund.

You are also going to have multiple retirement funds. Some you get passively, like a 401k that you do not contribute to, or social security, which is out of your control.

The real question should be, "How do I best allocate money among all the available retirement funds, and how do I best manage the money within these accounts?" Don't focus on the type of retirement vehicle itself. Instead, ask:

- "How much to I expect to have available from this account for use in retirement?"
- "How likely is it that I will achieve this goal?"
- "What is my back-up source of money if I don't achieve this goal?"

All these questions are more important that the type of retirement fund you are investing in.

The thrust of this book is to educate you about the nuances of many of the options, and alert you to hidden risks, so you can make educated decisions. I won't spend time explaining the obvious choices—there is a huge industry devoted to selling you products. The goal here is to help you find information you need to navigate among the choices wisely.

You want to learn how to supplement the passive plans with strong retirement plans that you control. See Chapter 2 and Chapter 9 for an in-depth discussion about retirement.

What are the best investments?

The best investments are the ones you understand and can explain to someone else. If you do not understand an investment, it is because:

- it does not make sense,
- it is not good, and
- the salesperson is not good.

Notice I use "and" and not "or." You are capable of understanding any investment that is appropriate for you. A good salesperson can explain any investment, no matter how complicated, so that you can understand it. A bad investment never has a good, understandable explanation.

Avoid salespeople who say, "Trust me" or "it is not important for you to know that" or "it will all work itself out."

The largest life insurance company in North America specifically trains its salespeople to not explain clearly how their products work. That is why they are the largest. If clients actually understood how the products work, then they wouldn't buy them, because there are many better products, in most of the categories they offer. Bring me any of their policies, and I will show you what you do not understand, explain it to you, and let you see other options that are better values. (For the rare product they have that actually suits you best, I'll just explain it to you, and encourage you to buy it.)

What are the riskiest investments?

The riskiest investments are the ones you do not understand. You should never own any of these. Every investment has some element of risk. Your challenge is to blend them so that you are comfortable with the combined risk, and that you have a nearly risk-free cushion for the income you need. My goal is to educate you, so that you never take on risk unknowingly. The only one who can answer the question "What are the riskiest investments for me" is you.

Should you rent or buy?

The facts are easy to assemble; the conclusion is hard to reach. The reason for this difficulty is that at some point, it becomes an emotional decision, not a factual one, and emotional decisions may not have just one correct answer.

On a factual level, just put the numbers together. Don't forget to account for tax savings on mortgage interest, and deductions for property taxes. But also don't forget to allow for unexpected costs associated with each option. There are numerous websites that will run you through the financial analysis.

If you are planning to hold onto a home for a long time, say fifteen years or more, your main deciding factor should be affordability. Will you be able to make monthly mortgage payments, even under adverse circumstances? If the answer is "No," don't buy, because homes are not easy to dispose of on short notice without suffering a loss. In a long-range situation, the current price (accounting for the work you need to do to move in), be it at the high end of the market or the low end, is less important than affordability. For shorter holding periods, the more important question is, "How much will you lose if you need to sell quickly, and is it worth taking the chance?"

On an emotional level, it is a matter of what are you willing to pay above and beyond the cost of renting, to satisfy the perceived psychological benefits of owning. If it is worth it to you, then buy. That is why you spend your time earning money—to spend it one what you value. (In the extremely rare situation where renting is more expensive, even considering all the risk and uncertain costs of buying, then the answer is obvious—just buy. But I'd be hard pressed to find a case like this.)

What is the best way to get a mortgage?

Look for the lowest total of all the money you will pay out over time. Shop all over—rates differ. If you go through a bank, realize that they may only offer you a few of their own products, which may not be the most competitive. If you go through a broker or loan originator, you may be able to save money, even after fees.

Also, consider the competency of the people you are working with, and their motivation. In-house bank loan officers gets paid whether you show up or not. Their job is to take applications and pass them on for approval. Independent brokers/originators are only paid if your loan closes. They are highly motivated to make the deal happen for you. They also have wider access to funders.

Good brokers/originators have the experience and organization to collect all the necessary paperwork, submit it, and respond quickly to lender questions. If you work with a company that has a great success rate getting mortgages approved on a timely basis, you know they do a good job. Lenders are eager to lend, when all the conditions have been met. That is how they make money.

Time is of the essence in real estate transactions. If you don't get the loan on time, you may not be able to get an extension on your closing date, and you can lose your deposit, and therefore lose the house. You need to work with a broker or lender who can really deliver. It does not do you any good to work with a bank that accepts and application without pre-screening it to measure the likelihood of being approved.

I know. I have a mortgage loan originator license, and I broker loans on a regular basis. It has to be done right.

What are common stock market and investment myths to be alert for?

Myth: The 60/40 theory or whatever ratio you use: According to legend, the ratio between fixed income instruments and equities is supposed to follow some predetermined ratio based on your age and longevity. Nonsense. There may be good guidelines based on age, but the real question is how to make sure that your "must have" expenses will be met so that you do not run out of money. That will determine your ratio.

Myth: The 4% rule states that as long as you do not take out more than 4% of your assets every year, you will be fine in retirement. That may have worked once, when portfolios regularly returned well in excess of 4%. But this rule has not been valid for more than a decade. So do not rely on it. For absolute safety, use 2%. That is a very conservative number, and it will scare you, because it means that if you have $2,000,000 in assets that produce income or growth, you can only be certain of $40,000 a year being available for you to spend. But I'd rather be scared than broke.

Myth: 8% hypothetical return is an abused term. Life insurers encourage you to confuse "hypothetical" with "average" return. An "average" return means that on average, over a long period of time, a portfolio will yield an average return of 8%. "Hypothetical" means "in theory" or "let's pretend." A hypothetical rate of return for 10, 20, 30, 50, or 70 years means returning exactly 8% each and every year for 10, 20, 30, 50, or 70 years. Never 7.99% and never 8.01%. Yet insurers show hypothetical returns and encourage you to think they mean average returns. "Hypothetical" never happens. "Hypothetical" returns never occur. The actual return will be more, or less. The long list of numbers on insurance projections labeled hypothetical may just as well be labeled "absolutely certain not to be accurate." Evaluate them accordingly.

Myth: Historical performance is another meaningless industry favorite. You know what it means—the name says it all. It is what happened in the past. What does that have to do with what will happen in the future? The marketplace is totally different than it was 20, 30, and 40 years ago. Back then, news travelled slowly. Markets closed, investors digested the results overnight, made decisions, and placed trades the next day. Today, many markets operate around the clock, decisions are made in fractions of a second by computers, and trades happen instantly. Fake news abounds, and market swings are wild. Investor panic and irrational optimism is unabated. Many investors are actually gamblers. They seek to take advantage of unsophisticated players who make mistakes. Don't confuse market performance and behavior in the past, before cell phones, Internet, social media, etc., with what is likely to happen today.

Chapter 21

NINE WAYS TO MAKE YOUR MONEY GROW

#1: Take Advantage of Time

IF YOU PUT ASIDE $100 a month and invest it in a tax-free account that pays 5% compounded interest, in ten years you will have $15,792. If you stop putting any more money aside at that point, in twenty more years you will have $43,180, which is nearly triple.

What you are doing is accessing the power of compounding.

Invest a small amount today, and it will grow a little in one year. The next year it grows the same amount, but the earnings from the first year grow as well. In the third year, your original money still grows the same amount, but now the earnings from the two previous years grow as well.

Looking at it by decade, the first 10 years show slow growth. The next 10 years do a little better. After that, it really takes off.

Now let's say you got into the habit of putting aside $100 a month. Maybe you do this by bringing a thermos of home brewed coffee to Starbucks every day, so you can enjoy the ambiance, look incredibly cool, and not spend any money. Or maybe you find a non-trendy café for breakfast, where you spend $5 instead of $10. Or maybe you slow down the pace of after-work drinks at happy hour. Or self park. Or clip coupons. Or read the news online. Or don't buy soft drinks in convenience stores—buy in bulk, keep them at home, and grab one when you leave. Etc.

After ten years, you will have probably gotten used to not having the designer coffee. If you keep putting away the $100 a month for an additional twenty years, you will have $84,648. So now you've never had the designer coffee, but you can own a motorboat and vacation home on a lake, in thirty years, free and clear. So you can either drink a cup of expensive coffee a day for the next thirty years, or you can have a vacation home. It's your choice.

Later we'll discuss how you can consistently earn 5%, tax-free, on your money for thirty years.

#2: Make a Budget.

Know what is coming in and going out.

The biggest reason people get into financial trouble is that they spend more than they make.

Obviously.

Everyone knows this, but most people pretend it doesn't apply to them.

Your adult life is divided into two parts—the years you earn money by working, and the years you earn money from income on investments and retirement funds. (If you are good at saving, you can even start the passive income early, while you are still working.) Next, list all the money you earn. Sort it into two groups— the money you make by working (that is, the money that comes in as a result of your efforts), and the money you earn from investments (passive income that comes in whether you go to work or not). Then figure out how to increase each.

Your goal is maximize each type of income and minimize expenses.

The difference gets put into investments. It sounds simple, and it is, but most people don't do it. Some people think they can go to a financial planner, who will wave a magic wand and come up with a plan for them. Which is what a financial planner does. (That is, come up with a plan, not wave a wand.) But they are going to start with this same exercise: List your income. List your expenses. If you are not making more than you spend, they will kick you out of their office. Because no magic wand is going to create a stream of income that is not being spent, which is what you need to do in order to have a financial plan.

If you don't know how much you are spending, and how much you are making, you can't save, and you can't put money aside. You need to know the numbers, and you need to spend less than you make. Only then can you develop a plan.

When I lived in New York on 24th Street, and worked on 49th, I would often walk to and from work on nice days. I passed about six Korean grocery shops. They always had a nice display of fruit outside, and it was easy to shop for a healthy dinner on the way home. The avenue in front of my apartment was one way, uptown. When I took the bus home on rainy days, I ended up on the downtown avenue, one block east. I discovered that produce there was five to ten cents cheaper per item. A 3rd Avenue apple might cost sixty cents; on 2nd Avenue it was fifty or fifty-five cents. A few items a day could mean a fifty cents or one dollar savings. I lived there for four years. When I left, one of the grocers on 3rd Avenue had bought up most of the buildings on the block. The guy on 2nd Avenue was still renting. Surprised?

#3. Prioritize Your Spending, and Budget Carefully

There are two ways to have more money. One is to earn more. The other is to spend less. Earning more is the harder of the two.

The goal of the first part of your life (working) is to make sure there is enough money in the second part (retirement with passive income) to live the way you want to live. The added challenge is to wisely invest the surplus between what you earn and what you spend, during the first part of your life.

Spending more than you earn? That's your choice. But unless you are anticipating an inheritance or windfall, or are expecting to die young, be prepared for a lifestyle constrained by lack of money. Does this sound harsh? Too bad. It's true. You have two choices— learn it now, or learn it later, when it is harder (but not impossible) to repair your finances.

Don't like reading this? Fine, go see a Disney movie—one of the happy ones. Then re-read the above paragraphs. Pick the story you believe is true, and run with it. (Hint: Some Disney movies are called fables for a reason.)

Budgeting: It is really simple. Go to any free website, and get a list of all the possible expense categories. Plug in what you spend monthly. Be realistic. If you don't know, start keeping track of each dollar. If you are spending more than you earn, figure out how to earn more, or where you can cut.

#4. Avoid Paying Taxes.

Make the government give you money. It's easy, and it is legal. In 1913, the government first got the idea that it would be a great thing to charge people a tax on their income. Before that, taxes were imposed different ways—licenses, fees, taxes on certain goods, taxes on property, taxes on estates, etc. In some years, income tax rates soared—in the 1930s they went as high as 90% of earned income! Although the rate came way back down, it has gradually been creeping up again. And more taxes have been added—sales tax has been steadily growing.

States and cities have added income taxes, and more and more products, like gasoline, tobacco, and alcohol have additional excise taxes of their own. Parks used to be free, and now some charge admission. It seems like everything is taxed. And that's because it is. Even if you are in the lowest income tax bracket, you end up paying a hefty amount in total taxes—often upwards of 50% of your income. When you die, you can get whacked again, with estate taxes. And just in case you've figured out a way to reduce your taxes, the government makes you calculate them another way—the alternative minimum tax—to see if they can get you to pay more anyhow. That's the price you pay for living in a great country like ours (and it is worth it). But the tax code, all ten thousand plus pages of it, contains hidden gems. There are many ways to reduce taxes—in effect, getting the government to give you money, instead of the other way around. You just have to know how to play the game.

Essentially, there are three ways to handle taxes:
- You can pay as you go
- You can defer them until later
- You can make them go away

Everyone is familiar with pay as you go—that's what happens when you buy anything, or when you file annual tax returns.

Most people are familiar with deferring taxes—IRA's, 401k's, pension plans, annuities, etc. By investing or squirreling away money in a manner approved by Congress, you get to put off paying some taxes until later in life, when presumably, your income will be lower, and your taxes will be lower. But there are two caveats you need to be aware of:

1. If you manage your finances right, you can continue to pull in nice hefty earnings until late in life, so your tax rate might not drop at all, and

2. Who knows what tax rates will be in the future?

So that leaves us with the third option—investing money in a manner that is exempt from federal income tax—money that grows tax-free, and comes to you or your heirs income tax-free. As of now, there are only two vehicles to do this—Roth accounts, and life insurance.

#5. Protect Your Assets.

What's the point of making money if someone can just take it away from you?

It's not as dumb a question as it sounds. Until a little over a hundred years ago, the vast majority of all people on Earth were born poor, lived poor, and died poor. There were very few rich people, and they spent a lot of their wealth building castles with moats, hiring armies to attack potential enemies, and making sure that the people around them never accumulated enough money to take any time off from work, thus effectively preventing potential threats. Almost everyone worked every day, and they consumed all that they grew, traded, or crafted, with nothing left over. You got to stop working when you either:

- Died,
- Got too sick to work, in which case, unless someone gave you food, you died
- Worked in vain, such as when disease or weather destroyed your crops or livestock, and you suddenly had no food, in which case, you got too sick to work, or starved, and then died.

The whole idea of retirement was a notion available to the select few—the powerful, and those who inherited wealth and also had the strength to defend it. Well into the 1900s nearly all people led a subsistence lifestyle, surviving from one harvest, hunt, or paycheck until the next. But starting in the 1900s, a large middle class emerged—ordinary people who were able to earn more than it cost to live. They were able to put something away for the future, consume less than they made, and amass modest assets or even wealth. Suddenly, people had savings, and with that came the idea that these assets, if unprotected, could be taken away. That is when the modern concept of insurance as asset protection was born.

It may seem obvious, because insurance is so ubiquitous, but most insurance is a modern phenomenon:

- You have homeowners insurance, because you put a large down payment on your home, and if it blows away, floods, or catches fire, and you have to rebuild, you'll have a source of funds to do so. If you don't have insurance, you'll still owe the bank money, but you will have lost your down payment and will be homeless. (If you don't own, you have renters insurance, which protects the stuff in the home you rent.)
- You have health insurance, so that you can afford medical care if you get sick.
- You have car insurance because the most likely way that you are going to get physically hurt in life is with an automobile, and because the most likely way that you will hurt someone else is with an automobile; if you don't have insurance, you

may be held liable, and the person you hurt will be able to take away your assets.

- You have umbrella insurance, in case someone gets a judgment against you that is larger than the liability insurance you carry on your home or car.

Plus, some insurance is creditor protected (notably some life insurance and annuities), which means that you can put assets in an insurance policy and know that if something bad happens—you hurt someone, you go bankrupt, you borrow money and cannot repay—it will remain yours. The more you have in protected assets, the more you get to keep and use, no matter what happens to you. Everything else—real estate, businesses, your gold coin collection, the money under your mattress, your bank accounts, and your prized first edition, signed baseball card collection—can all be taken away.

#6. Read the Ads.

And after, don't believe what you read. Acquire knowledge.

Here's the catch. People and businesses that are trying to get you to spend (your) money (at their place of business) have become very clever at figuring out what makes people want to spend money. And they know how to push just the right buttons to get you to part with that money. Mainly, they promise you benefits that are worth more than you spend.

Sometimes the benefits are real. Some toothpaste may get your teeth sparklier than others, and some detergents may make your clothes cleaner. But whiter teeth are not likely to make you more popular, attractive, or successful in business. And dull white shirts won't be your ruination. Sure, while a bright smile may get you a tiny edge in being noticed, or sharp clothing may provoke a slightly warmer welcome, chances are that unless your grin is repulsive or your outfit slovenly, it is not going to make much of a difference in the long run. Same with a car. Or a purse. Or a brand of liquor. It doesn't matter. While the product may be "better" than a competitor's, the extra, intangible benefits are probably not going to materialize.

The same is true for other products and services. In the 1980s, there was an investment firm called E.F. Hutton. Their slogan was: "When E.F. Hutton talks, people listen." It was well known, and they spent millions associating this slogan with their brand. People still remember it. (Ask any 60 year old what happens when E.F. Hutton talks, and they'll tell you, "People listen.") The Hutton ads showed people in crowded, noisy rooms, and when one person said to another, "My broker is E.F Hutton, and he says…" the whole room fell silent. The implication is that the speaker was getting better investment advice than anyone else in the room because his advisor was E.F. Hutton. (It also implied that the speaker was a smarter person as well.) Never heard of E. F. Hutton? It was founded in 1904 and became one of the largest and most respected financial firms in the country.

In 1980, one enterprising E. F. Hutton branch manager figured out that if he wrote a large check for more than the branch had available, and deposited it in another bank, it would take a few days to clear. (This was 1980, after all, and computers were slower and clunkier, and a lot of banks still used paper transactions.) He could cover this check a few days later with another one, and keep the process going forever. He advised headquarters of his scheme, which netted his branch an extra profit of $30,000 a month, and within three years, the firm was doing this with $250 million a day.

When one bank caught on and notified the U.S. Attorney, Hutton denied the practice at first, then pleaded guilty to 2,000 charges of wire and mail fraud, and paid a penalty of over $10 million in 1985. In 1987, an internal probe revealed that one branch was laundering money for the Mafia, and the government prepared to indict the firm.

As luck would have it (or not), the next week, in October 1987, the market crashed, and Hutton lost $76 million, and the investigation got sidetracked. When Hutton merged with another firm in early 1988, it was revealed that Hutton had been facing massive cash shortages since 1985 and had been secretly up for sale since 1986. Several mergers later, the name is gone, and now, conversations don't stop when people mention E.F. Hutton.

While they were around, they did no better or worse for clients than other similar firms. If you had your investments with them, you may have felt that you were better off. You weren't. So the lesson is: read the ads. They have valuable information. But be skeptical. If a benefit seems unrealistic, it probably is. If claims can't be substantiated, they're probably illusory. With all the access you have to the Internet to easily check facts, shame on you if you fall for the hype. It costs money to advertise. The only money these firms earn comes from the money you give them to manage. The more advertising you see, the higher their expenses are. Which means that your gains are lower.

#7. Be Skeptical.

You are going to read and hear two types of advisory messages: advertising and expert opinions. Advertising is paid for by people who have a vested interest in having you believe what they are saying. The information stated may or may not be true. Some industries, like insurance, are highly regulated, so there actually are very good chances that the advertising information is accurate. But they are still trying to get you to buy something. The products they are pushing might be good products; but they might not be good for you, or good for you at this point in time, or the best for you. They just might be great for someone else who sees or hears that same ad.

Either way, you are going to have to make that determination yourself, based on your knowledge, and based on the advice you sift through. The appropriateness of expert opinions for you has similar problems. The experts may be smart, and their recommendations good for some people, but unless they know who you are, and what your needs are, they have no way of broadcasting a message that is accurate for all their listeners. And if you are dealing one-on-one with an expert, they are either being paid an hourly fee to advise you, or a commission, which means they don't get paid if you don't buy. In the first case, you don't know how much the expert knows, and you don't know if he knows what is right for you, and in the second case, well, do you think that a commissioned salesperson is unbiased? When I sell insurance, I work on a commission basis. And I have to force myself to try to think independently, without biases that I naturally pick up by reading professional literature. I'm not sure all my contemporaries fight the same fight—it is too easy to just push the product that is easiest to sell, pays the most, or that you are most familiar with.

Also, when you read so-called independent write-ups or hear investigative reports, who do you think is doing the writing or reporting? An expert? No, writers and reporters do it. They call people who they think might be experts (like me) to ask questions and get input for their stories. (I understand this too well—I get calls all the time.) They are not experts themselves on the issues; they are just expert writers and reporters. So the story that gets produced is not always accurate or impartial. I know—I read them daily and shake my head at the advice given. I have a burgeoning file of stories I've collected from respected financial publications, offering what is just plain old bad and wrong advice.

The best thing about living in the Internet age is that you can check out anything online. Someone is always out there offering advice, information, and instruction, and someone else is always there with a rebuttal. It's amazing how much is out there, and it's surprising how often people don't use the resources. Want a better explanation of anything I've discussed in this book? Google it! A client of mine called attention to a full-page ad in the local paper, which costs about $10,000 to run, touting the services of a particular investment advisor, and guaranteeing 9.5% returns. So I Googled the name, and the first thing that pops up is a story on how he was disbarred in Nevada and Pennsylvania. Then came stories about lawsuits against him. Then came his website, with glowing praise, and not even a word about the administrative actions pending against him in twenty states, which I had just learned from reading the headlines of the links that popped up—without ever opening a page!

Was this man stupid—paying $10,000 for an ad when he had such a blemished record? Didn't he know that people would check on him, and that he would never get a dollar's worth of business from his investment in advertising? I got my answer the following month, when he ran the ad again. He figured, correctly, that enough people would not even do basic, minimal research, and he made so much money the first time he ran the ad that he felt it was worthwhile to do it again. Then I found an article published by a law firm that claims that more than 40,000 retirees and seniors attend his seminars every year. It quotes a Bloomberg article (9/11/2007—Susan Antilla): "He is a former lawyer with a checkered past… Resigned from the Florida Bar in 1997 after receiving two consecutive 6-month suspensions on the heels of four previous public disciplines…"

#8. Find Advisors Who Are Smarter Than You.

Don't take what they say at face value—ask questions. Make them prove that they understand the products they sell, and why those products are right for you. Avoid canned sales pitches—make them explain what they are proposing in their own words. Take financial advice from people you respect. Demand proof of the claims they make. If you don't understand something, make them explain it to you until you do. It has to make sense for it to be real. Don't be fooled by numbers and charts—understand the claims being made.

If claims are too good to be true, they probably aren't true. If they are wildly different from claims competitors are making, they are probably not accurate.

There are only two possibilities with financial products if they promise a lot more than anyone else: either they are losing money, or lying. If they are losing money, they won't be around for very long, so you'll never get the returns promised. And if they're lying, well… you read the newspapers, don't you? Insurance is a highly regulated industry. And for good reason. There are lots of disclosures. Read them.

#9. Wear X-Ray Goggles.

Not literally. But pretend you are. Why are you being shown something? What's behind that recommendation? What's the reason your advisor feels this product is the most appropriate one for you? Why is one product being recommended over another? There is a huge range of financial products available.

One person can only be familiar with a portion of them. It is the natural inclination of a salesperson to find several products that they like, become familiar with them, and recommend them to their clients. They usually do this with the best of intentions—they've done the research, and they've found something that appeals to them, so they use it.

What you bring to the discussion is an intimate knowledge of your needs, preferences, and concerns—something that no one else knows. There may be products out there that your advisor is not familiar with that would better address your needs. You may need to find them yourself, or direct your advisor to look for them. The value of wearing x-ray goggles is that you can use them to tell if a product is right for you. When in doubt, ask. If you don't get answers that make sense, insist until you get them, or leave.

Are the benefits being offered real, or illusory? Feeling good is wonderful, but understanding why you are feeling good is even better. It's no shame to say, "I don't understand this." If it can't be explained to you, you either have the wrong product, or the wrong teacher. The financial crisis of 2008/2009 was caused in large part by people (sophisticated and intelligent) trading financial instruments they did not understand.

Don't rely on the government to protect you. Yes, they will pass laws to outlaw people doing bad things to you, but only after a pattern emerges. Yes, they will prosecute bad people, but only after the damage is done. Bad people will always figure their way around protective barriers—if you don't go opened-eyed into every financial presentation, you run the risk of being the case that causes the government to react, only after you have been hurt. Sure, it will help others in the future, but not you. Even good, well-intentioned advisors may not come up with the best products for you, unless you can help them evaluate the appropriateness of what they recommend for your situation.

APPENDICES
&
REFERENCES

Appendix 1

TIPS ON HAVING UNCOMFORTABLE CONVERSATIONS WITH YOUR PARENTS

O NE OF THE HARDEST CONVERSATIONS adults have with their parents is the inevitable "what do you want when you get older, and how can I be of help?"

But these conversations are crucial, because, at some point, the care of your parents may fall on you, and the better prepared you are, the better the outcome will be.

There are also financial implications for you as well. I won't go into this now, but when it comes to designing your retirement, the possible future expense of caring for your parents, or other relatives, has to be considered.

Usually, the "talk" doesn't happen until the first funeral of a contemporary of theirs, which, ironically, can make it easier, because, suddenly, the questions are real and not just theoretical. But it could also be too late to start the conversation. Ideally, you want to ease into it, over time, using opportunities that arise naturally for different topics.

I've talked dozens of clients through what I call the "big boy/ big girl" talk, which is essentially the following, phrased more diplomatically:

"Mom, Dad: I know you think of me as your little child, and I'll always be your child, but I'm a big boy/girl now, and I'd like to be helpful to you as you get older, just like you helped me grow up. I'd like to get your thoughts on…" and here you can pick anything and everything below.

But BEFORE you do this, determine who else should be in on the conversations, or aware of them (i.e. your siblings, their siblings, etc.)

AND if you want the conversations to go well, honestly address the following issues before you open your mouth:

1. Recognize that the conversation is for the benefit of all of you; it is not just for you, and it is not just for your parents. Choose language that reflects that.
2. Recognize that this is a new part of your relationship. There will be disagreements—that is okay. When disagreements do come up, make it clear that that it is okay to disagree.
3. Understand that your parents have the right to be in control of their own lives, even if you think they should be making different decisions. If you end up financially caring for your parents, it does not give you the right to make decisions for them (except, possibly, in matters of safety).
4. Be prepared to LISTEN. No matter how carefully you choose your words, they might be misunderstood. Be prepared to spend a lot of time listening.
5. Treat your parents with respect. It's one of the Ten Commandments, and it is also the only way to get meaningful results.
6. Be prepared to revisit questions and answers over time. Things change.

Topics to discuss are:

Money:
- ❑ Will they need your help in retirement if they are healthy?
- ❑ Will they need your help in retirement if they are ill?
- ❑ Are they taking care of anyone (other child, other relative, etc.) and will that obligation be passed on to you?

Wishes:
- ❑ Where do they want to live while they are taking care of themselves?
- ❑ Where do they want to live when they need physical assistance in caring for themselves?
- ❑ Who do they want making medical decisions for them if they cannot make them for themselves?

Records:
- ❑ Where are their documents located? Where are their password lists located?
- ❑ Where are the three key documents, and what do they say? (Durable Power of Attorney—who makes decisions for them if they cannot make them for themselves, while they are alive; Health Care Surrogate—who makes medical decisions if they cannot; Living Will—what are their end of life wishes?) You should also know where the Will is, but there is little in there that you need to know while they are alive.
- ❑ If they don't have these, they need to make them. It is not fair to you or them to leave this unresolved.
- ❑ Where are all the documents that confirm what they've told you about insurance, assets, etc.?

THE BUSY PERSON'S GUIDE TO LIFE AFTER ONE'S WORKING YEARS

"I don't have time to read a long, complicated book about retirement, long-term care, investments, and taxes. Can't you just quickly tell me what I need to know? And don't confuse me with rates of return, projections, hypothetical performances, etc."

SURE I CAN. THE OVERVIEW is simple. It's the details that get more complicated, but you don't need to think about them now. (I put them at the end of this booklet in case you want to read them.) If you understand the basic concept, we'll provide you with all the other information you need later.

Three stages of retirement:

Chances are that your life in retirement will be almost as long as the time you spent working. It is not uncommon for people to live into their 90's, so if you retire at 65, you could have thirty more years ahead of you. Thirty years without earned income. What are you going to do for money in those three decades?

Let's break down those decades of retirement into three distinct spans of time, for the purpose of budgeting.

The early years: You are active, robust, in good health, and vigorously pursuing the storybook retirement lifestyle. You may travel widely, engage in a variety of hobbies, and spend money on what used to be leisure time activities, but now occupies your entire time.

The middle years: You have begun to slow down. You are not as active as before. You may travel less. You spend more time dealing with medical issues that come as part of entering old age. But you are still mainly independent and get around without much assistance. You just don't travel as much as you used to.

The later years: You are officially old. Attention to medical issues takes up a significant amount of your time. You may need substantial assistance in performing daily tasks. You may not be able to care for yourself at all, and you may move to a long-term care facility, or create something similar at home. In the transition to this phase, you may have a major medical episode that puts you in rehab for a while. But not necessarily—the transition can be gradual. (If it is sudden, you've essentially skipped the middle years. So it is key that your financial planning allows for this possibility.)

Expenses during retirement:

Next, let's look at expenses during each of those time periods, and divide those expenses into three categories.

You know that you definitely need to have money for your necessary expenses, and it would be nice to have money for your discretionary expenses as well. The emergency funds are what will keep you out of poverty if you incorrectly budget in the first two areas.

	Early Years	Middle Years	Later Years
Necessary Expenses			
Food	High	Moderate	Low
Housing	High	High	Low
Healthcare/ Custodial Care	Low	Moderate	High
Insurance	High	High	Moderate
Clothing	High	Moderate	Low
Taxes	High	Moderate	Low
Utilities	High	High	Low
Transportation	High	Moderate	Low
Debt Repayment	High	Moderate	Low
Upkeep	High	Moderate	Low
Discretionary Expenses			
Travel	High	Moderate	None
Entertainment	High	Moderate	None
Dining Out	High	Moderate	None
Gifts	High	High	Varied
Recreation	High	Moderate	None
Emergency Funds	High	Moderate	Low

Preparing for retirement:

Clearly, in order to support your retirement, you have to prepare sufficient assets with particular attention to five factors:

- Your investments need to produce at least enough income for your necessary expenses.

- Your investments and guaranteed income need to increase at a rate greater than the rate of inflation to keep up with costs.
- You need to manage risk and uncertainty, so that your assets last your lifetime.
- You need security of principal, so you don't suffer market losses.
- You need to convert assets to income.

Where is retirement income going to come from?

By definition, retirement is the period during which you cease to actively earn income—all your income comes from passive activity, such as investments, pensions, social security, retirement accounts, etc.

The goal during your working years is to build each of these assets as high as you can. In retirement, the goal is to make sure that you have money in all these assets as long as you are alive. Since you do not know how long you will live, and you do not know exactly how costs will rise over time, the real goal is to make sure that every year, you do not spend more than the increase in the value of the assets, unless there is a mechanism for automatic replenishment.

Think of it as having various buckets of money. You want to keep your hands out of any bucket that is diminishing, so that it never empties.

Now, let's talk about the five main buckets that you will have. The most important are Buckets #1 and #5, and they need to cover your necessary expenses:

Bucket 1: Social Security, plus fully funded pensions and fixed annuities or deferred income annuities—solid, reliable assets that will produce income while you are alive.

Bucket 2: Tax-deferred investments, such as IRA's, 401k's, and the like—these assets will continue to grow without you having to pay income tax on the growth as long as it is not distributed. These will fluctuate in value, and the income they produce will fluctuate as well.

Bucket 3: Other investments—stocks and bonds in regular accounts, real estate, businesses, collectibles, loans you've made to people. These assets will fluctuate, plus if they earn income, you will need to pay income taxes immediately.

Bucket 4: Roth IRA's—these will fluctuate depending on how well you've invested the funds. The growth will never be taxable.

Bucket 5: Cash value life insurance. This will continue to increase as long as you pay premiums. Plus, it offers a unique feature that none of the other buckets have—you can spend most of the accumulated cash value, and this bucket will be automatically replenished in full or in part when you die. This means that you can enjoy the use of these funds while you are alive, knowing that after you die, they will be replenished for your heirs.

How do I decide which bucket to take money from?

These are the four possible financial scenarios that you will encounter in retirement:

1) Your investments are increasing, and income tax is low: This is when you want to go into Buckets #2 and #3. In addition to the regular income from Bucket #1, the income you pull out of #2 and #3 is going to be taxed at a low rate. Spend the growth in Buckets #2 and #3 on necessities and discretionary expenses, and build your emergency fund.

2) Your investments are increasing, and income tax is high: You are going to be paying more in income tax on the proceeds from Bucket #1, so you'll want to pull the money you need and want to spend from Bucket #4, the Roth accounts, because this will not increase your taxes. You can still pull money from Buckets #2 and #3, but you will net less, due to taxes.

3) Your investments are decreasing, and income tax is low: If you've planned Bucket #1 properly, you should be relying on this primarily for the necessary expenses. Go into IRAs, 401k, and the like in moderation, because the tax climate is favorable, but you don't want to deplete these assets any more than you have to. Get your discretionary funds from whichever bucket will incur the least damage.

4) Your investments are decreasing, and income tax is high: in addition to getting your regular income from Bucket #1, you'll want to leave every other bucket alone, except #5, the cash value whole life insurance. You can take money out without paying taxes and wait for it to replenish itself in the years when you use the other buckets.

Follow these rules, and you won't need to change your lifestyle when returns are down, or when interest rates are low. You will have money in the right places, so while your friends are worrying about rates of return, underperforming assets, and diminishing portfolios, you'll be set for life.

If you are concerned about having enough in each bucket, we can also look at long-term care insurance and disability insurance. They are both good ways of pooling risk, so that you are not entirely dependent on just your assets. This, however, is a separate discussion.

Appendix 3

RETIREMENT PLANNING ANALYSIS WORKSHEET

THE FIRST STEP IN PLANNING for retirement is to assemble information on your expected expenses, income, and assets. We'll start with the best estimates you currently have, and then make allowances for possible changes. We also need to know a little about your current income and spending habits.

It will also be helpful for you to have, in writing, a sense of the types of investments you are comfortable with.

If you are unsure about any answer, just use your best estimate, or give an approximate range.

If you have a spouse or partner with independent resources or income, or if you track your expenses and assets separately, please complete a separate worksheet for that person. If you do everything jointly, just use the spouse section below.

Personal Information:

Name: _____

Circle: Male or Female

Date of Birth: _____

Expected retirement age: _____

If currently employed/self-employed, estimated annual salary or earnings from working: $ _____

Do you currently spend more or less than this amount on ordinary expenses? ____More ____Less

How much per year? $ _____

If you spend less, where do you put the savings? _____

_____

If you spend more, where do you get the funds? ___ ⸱ _____

_____

Spouse or Partner Personal Information (if applicable):

Name: _____

Circle: Male or Female

Date of Birth: _____

Expected retirement age: _____

If currently employed/self-employed, estimated annual salary or earnings from working: $ _____

Do you currently spend more or less than this amount on ordinary expenses? ____More ____Less

How much per year? $ _____

If you spend less, where do you put the savings? _____

_____

If you spend more, where do you get the funds? _____

_____

Dependents:

List name and birthdate for each dependent you will need to support in your retirement, and your expected annual cost of support.

Name	Birthdate	Relationship	Annual	Projected Expense

Extra-ordinary considerations that you expect to affect income, assets, and expenses in your retirement. For example, sale of real estate, an expected inheritance, major gifts to children or grandchildren (such as helping them buy a home, or educational expense assistance). Try to estimate the amount and number of years these are expected.

Income from	Expense for	Reason	Amount	Approx. Date

Expected Retirement Expenses:

Housing: Mortgage or Rent (monthly) _____

Property Taxes (annually) _____

Condo fees (monthly) _____

Electric (monthly) _____

Gas (monthly) _____

Cable (monthly) _____

Phone (monthly) _____

Other Recurring Expenses (monthly) _____

Homeowners and Hurricane Insurance

(annually) _____

Food: Groceries (weekly) _____

Dining Out (weekly) _____

Health Care:

Private Insurance (monthly) _____

Medicare (monthly) _____

Co-pays (monthly) _____

Dental Insurance (monthly) _____

Hearing/Vision (monthly) _____

Drugs & Medical Supplies (monthly) _____

Insurance: Life Insurance (annually) _____
            Long-Term care Insurance (annually) _____
            Other Insurance (annually) _____
Personal: Clothing (monthly) _____
            Personal Expenses (monthly) _____
            Gifts (monthly) _____
            Donations (monthly) _____
            Entertainment/Recreation (monthly) _____
            Travel (monthly) _____
            Hobbies (monthly) _____
            Income Taxes (annually) _____
            Other (monthly) _____

Expected Retirement Income (monthly):

            Social Security _____
            Pension _____
            Annuity Income _____
            Work in Retirement _____
            Rental Income _____
            Other Investment Income _____
            Other _____

Retirement Savings/Investments:

Employer Sponsored Plans (401K, 403B, Sep, 457)
Value: Where Held:

IRA's (all types)
Value: Type: Where Held:

Stock and Bond Portfolio
Value: Type: Where Held:

Tax-Deferred Annuities
Value: Where Held:

Life Insurance
Value: Type: Where Held:

Cash, Savings Accounts, CD's
Value: Where Held:

Other
Value: Where Held:

Own Home
Value: Amount Owed:

Real Estate or Other Investments
Value: Where Held:

This list should be a complete inventory of everything you own, expect to come in, and expect to spend. Without it, you cannot plan a retirement budget.

The next step is to assess your tolerance for risk, which can be done online. Choose two or three calculators and see if you get comparable results.

The numbers above, in conjunction with your risk tolerance, will be used by you, or any financial advisor (or computer program) you choose to work with, to develop a plan.

The input is standard. Your challenge is to find someone you are comfortable with, who is experienced, and who is well recommended to help you look at the potential and reliability of whatever plans you come up with.

Appendix 4

THE "529 ENHANCED REPLACEMENT PLAN"

A COLLEGE SAVINGS PLAN WITH MORE BENEFITS AND NO DOWNSIDES

I F YOU ARE LOOKING TO save money for higher education, a traditional "529" plan is probably one of the worst ways to do it. Yet it is highly touted by investment advisors, because they are not familiar with the alternatives. (Another less-than-ideal way to save in Florida is the Florida Prepaid Plan, but let's leave that for later.)

A better way is what I call a "529 Enhanced Replacement Plan," which isn't a "529" plan at all.

But first, let's understand what a "529" plan is and what its drawbacks are.

What is a "529" plan? It varies by state, and the details vary, but the general concept is similar among all of them:

- Parents (and anyone else who wants to give a child a gift) put after-tax money (that is, money they have already reported as income and paid income taxes on) into a specially created investment account, and then hope it grows over time.

- If all the right conditions apply (and there are many), the child can use some or all of the money to pay for some school expenses. If the money has grown inside the plan over the years, like it is supposed to, there are no income taxes due on the gain, as long as it is spent on approved education expenses.

BUT,

- If you violate some of the rules, you can be heavily penalized, and taxed. This applies to how you put money in, how you take it out, and what you spend it on. What makes sense to you may not make sense to the government, and the government writes the rules.

- If you end up applying for financial aid of any sort, for any reason, the funds you've saved in a 529 plan can severely reduce the amount of your award.

- There is a limit as to what you can put in.

- The money in the 529 plan needs to be managed in order for it to grow. If managed poorly, the plan can lose value. Everything is usually invested in the stock market, and the stock market goes up and down. Even after a substantial number of years, there is no guarantee that you will have more money than you put in, and you could even have less. Some plans have high management fees, making it harder for your money to grow.

- There are dozens of ways to mess up a 529 plan.

"529" plans are essentially glorified investment accounts, dependent on stock market returns.

(A Florida Prepaid Plan, on the other hand, will at least return what you put in, with no interest, if you don't use it. But the amount you can put in is very limited, and so are the places where you can use the funds.)

My solution—the "529 Enhanced Replacement Plan." It is a way to save for college with none of the downsides of a "529" or "Prepaid" plan, with many advantages:

- The money is income tax-free coming out. (You use after-tax money to fund it, just like the other plans.)

- You can spend the money on whatever you want—college related, or not.

- You continue to have money in the plan AFTER college is over, and it continues to grow, so you can use it in middle age, or retirement, income tax-free.

- The growth is automatic, and guaranteed. It never loses value, and you don't have to manage it. Almost always, the growth exceeds the guarantee. But it always grows, every year, irrespective of the financial markets.

- You can put in an unlimited amount. You can decide how much to contribute, and when to contribute. You can do it all at once, or year by year, and vary the amount contributed.

- It doesn't count against you when you apply for financial aid or awards.

- There are very few rules.

- It is easy.

So why don't more people use this plan?

So why don't more people use this plan? Because it pays very little in commissions to those who sell it (so most advisors don't event bother to learn about it), many advisors are simply unaware of it, and it has to be designed correctly in order to work properly. Plus, it does not have a "sexy" name with numerals in it—this plan is basically a well designed guaranteed investment inside a life insurance framework. But it has to be designed specifically for each client. An advisor must be willing to work hard to create a structure that pays the lowest possible commission to the advisor, so that they can put more of your money to work for you.

Appendix 5

THE WHITE COLLAR PROFESSIONAL'S BILL OF RIGHTS

YOU HAVE SEVERAL COLLEGE DEGREES. You are bright. You are successful.

And you probably feel insulted the way salespeople approach you to try to sell you things—especially insurance and financial products.

I know I feel that way. I have degrees from Princeton and Wharton, and I found that when I needed to know the facts, all I found was a sales pitch. That is why I entered the field, after I had completed several successful careers in business.

These are your rights:

1. **The right to understand** the products you are considering buying, how they work, and what they will cost. Financial products are notoriously complex, in part by nature, and sometimes by design. Too often, clients tell me they don't understand what they own or why they own it. It is nothing to be ashamed of. But it can be changed. My pledge: meet with me, I will answer questions, explain things, and _promise_ not to ask you to buy something unless you initiate the request.

2. **The right to compare** similar, and different, products. Once you've seen two or three products side by side, you are bright enough to understand the differences, once they have been pointed out. You never buy anything else important without comparing—why should financial products be different?

3. **The right to get the greatest possible benefit** out of the money you spend. You are all too well aware that money is in short supply. Don't spend more than you need to. Whether buying new products or reviewing what you own, our goal should be to reduce cash outflow.

Appendix 6

WHAT HAPPENED TO GAIL'S $160,000?

G AIL, 60, HAD BEEN DIVORCED for many years and was about to retire. She was in a long-term relationship with a partner who was financially independent and helped with living expenses. She owned her own home, had some small investments, and a tenant who paid rent to her. She had two children, and several grandchildren, and wanted to accomplish three goals:

1. Have enough income for the rest of her life to live her current lifestyle, if she stays healthy.

2. Have enough income to take care of herself if she has a long period of declining health.

3. Leave money to her children and grandchildren when she passes away.

At the time, annuities were paying a good rate, so we rolled over a retirement fund into two annuities, with the plan to take income down the road a bit, perhaps after ten years or so. We also bought a small, traditional long-term care policy, because prices were still low on these, especially at her age, and the benefits were nice. She already had another policy that was much older, and that cost very little, and together, they made a nice cushion for the eventual possibility of poor health.

But annuities will only provide limited income, and the long-term care policies only paid benefits if she actually needed long-term care. She wanted something that could give her an income in twenty years or so, and provide the guarantee that her premiums would always produce a benefit for her, living or deceased (unlike, say, long-term care policies, or auto insurance, or homeowners insurance, or health insurance, where she might very well spend money on premiums for decades and never see a penny in return). She did not want to have to sell any of her small investments, which provided a good income.

Gail did not want her retirement income to be taxable (like a portion of the annuity payments and any required minimum distributions from some of the remaining retirement accounts). She especially did not want to get socked with income taxes when she died, so she could leave everything to the children without having it disappear in taxes.

She wanted an investment that would grow in time, tax-free, that she could add more money to when she wanted, and also have the flexibility to not add money to in future years, that would give her a cushion of money she could go to for roof repairs, a cruise, a new kitchen, a new car, or the like, without paying income taxes. She also wanted to have it build into something that she could leave, income tax-free, when she passed.

So we bought a traditional whole life insurance policy (not one of the fancy variables or universals) and designed it so that there was a base premium and an optional additional premium that allowed her to increase premiums when she wanted, with funds that would nearly 100% go toward increasing the tax-free cash value. In some years she would pay a substantial premium, and in others, much less. She herself determined what she wanted to contribute, not the insurance company. Essentially, it was a place to park extra money so it could grow into a long-term tax-free retirement fund and an estate, on top of what she already had. The idea was that, twenty or twenty-five years down the road, when she was 80 or 85, she would have a considerable amount of cash available to her, tax-free, to use while she was alive, and a nice size death benefit, tax-free, for her children and grandchildren to receive in another fifteen or twenty-five years when she eventually passed away.

What we did was we took out a whole life insurance policy that gives the option of putting in between $12,000 and $20,000 a year in premiums, pays dividends that could eventually pay the premiums, has tax-free income available, and offers a nice size death benefit for her children.

Eight years later, and Gail has invested $160,000 into the policy, and the cash value, should she decide to surrender it, is about the same. The death benefit, now, is over $500,000. But at 68, she has a long life ahead of her. She is scaling down her annual premiums to $12,000, but she could even afford to stop contributing altogether and still have substantial benefits. We're still on track for looking at taking out money starting in about twelve years, if the need is there, when the cash value is well over $400,000, and the death benefit is over $700,000. But Gail may stop putting money in sooner, or decide to put in less, or even go back to the $20,000 a year. Perhaps she'll decide to keep adding funds and end up with millions in cash value and death benefits.

But no matter what she decides, she knows for sure that she has met her financial goals. She is adequately protected in case she needs long-term care, she has enough taxable income to meet her needs, and she has repositioned $160,000 over the past 8 years, moving it from low-yielding accounts and risky stock funds to a safe, consistent, easy accessible, tax-free resource that will:

1. Give her enough supplemental income for the rest of her life if she wants it

2. Still have enough income from the long-term care policies to take care of her if she has a long period of declining health.

3. Let her leave money to her children and grandchildren when she passes away.

Appendix 7

THE NINE JOURNEYS OF A
SUCCESSFUL ADULT

What distinguishes an adult from a child? It is not size, or age, because we all know plenty of bigger, older people who appear to be adults but who haven't really gotten the hang of it.

Of course, there's no magic turning point when a child becomes an adult, and, as an adult, if you really want to fulfill your potential as a human being, you are constantly growing, learning, and evolving. It never ends, except at death.

But at some point, you realize that you are more or less successful at being an adult, and more comfortable than not at wearing the mantle of adulthood.

The change happens when you've moved along sufficiently on each of nine journeys that encompass your life. Success happens when you reach a certain comfort level in each journey, and you continue to grow.

One: Journey to Financial Independence

Children are dependent on their parents or others for support. Adults support themselves. Successful adults have a plan in place to cover all the possible situations that may arise: disability, illness, early death, longevity in retirement, and responsibility for supporting others. You may never have "enough" money, or get everything you want, but you will be a successful adult if you are on a trajectory to being financially secure. In order to do that, you need to be knowledgeable about finances, planful about saving and insuring yourself, and well-informed enough to cut through all the garbage people try to sell you to pick what is beneficial to you, and not to them.

Two: Journey to Mature Family Relationships

As a child, you have a set of relationships with parents, siblings, and extended family that are reinforced year after year, and mimicked by the relationships your siblings have with parents and extended family. A child focuses on him or herself. The relationship with the older generation is hierarchical—you are less powerful than the older generation, you are the creation of the older generation, and they are your teachers. As an adult, you need to shift into relationships with that generation as one adult to another, and also consider your relationships with your siblings and cousins as adult-to-adult. You may even have to become the caregiver to the generation that raised you, and to some extent, "parent" them. When you are comfortable in that role, leaving behind the childhood pettiness, resentment, admiration, jealousies, and shifting into dealing with each other as adults, you've successfully transitioned into being an adult.

Three: Journey to Self-Sustaining Peer Relationships

Relationships between children are buffered by the presence of disciplining adults. Relationships between adult peers are successful when you learn to respect others and resolve differences without outside authority figures. You need to be able to see situations from the perspective of others, and not just that of yourself, and figure out amicable ways of getting along and resolving differences.

Four: Journey to Exclusive Relationships (This journey is optional)

As an adult, you can choose to get into an exclusive, mutual relationship with another adult (such as marriage, partnering, monogamous cohabitation, etc.). The defining characteristics of such a relationship can be sexual exclusiveness, parenting children, or financial interdependence. You can go from one exclusive relation to another, serially. A few people can maintain simultaneous exclusive relationships, parceling out which piece of each relationship is exclusive (but this is very hard to do). Or you can remain single/independent and still be a successful adult. The key is to maintain equilibrium whether you're in a relationship or by yourself.

Five: Establishing Mentoring Relationships

Successful adults are able to give back to others, teaching what they learned in life.

Six: Seeking One's Potential

Successful adults are continually working to develop the potential within them.

Seven: Developing Perspective

Successful adults continually reassess their views of the world around them, incorporating what they learn and what they experience to reinterpret what they see so it makes more sense. They use new knowledge to function well in their relationships with others.

Eight: Crafting A Legacy

The final measure of success is when you leave a legacy of your values that exists without you being present. It is the only certain determinant of success, and it is bittersweet, because you will never be sure that you have achieved it (although you should have many indications of the probability that this will occur).

Nine: Embracing Failure

As a child, failure is seen often as a negative thing, with negative consequences. Too often, when a child fails at something, he or she interprets (or is told) that he or she is a failure, and not that he or she has simply failed at a task or activity. The successful adult has learned to:

- Differentiate between failing at something and being a failure,
- Use failure as an opportunity to learn,
- Recognize that everyone fails at something at some point in time, and that it does not diminish one's worth as a person,

- Take responsibility for failure, and the consequences, if any,
- Apologize for damage caused, and make amends,
- And change behavior

WHAT IS THE DIFFERENCE BETWEEN WHOLE LIFE INSURANCE, TERM INSURANCE, AND ALL THE REST

VARIABLE LIFE INSURANCE, UNIVERSAL LIFE INSURANCE, AND THE OTHER FLAVORS OF "PERMANENT" OR "CASH VALUE" LIFE INSURANCE?

Life Insurance in General:

THE ACTUAL COST TO THE company to pay claims rises as the client ages.

Companies charge more than the actual cost of insurance so they can bank and invest the difference to meet this rising cost over time, while keeping premiums the same.

If they do not collect enough of a difference, or the money is not profitably invested, either the policy expires, or they need to raise premiums to cover the difference.

Term Life:

You can pay the actual cost of insurance, which rises every year. This is called an annually renewable term policy. Or you pay an average cost over a particular term (like 10, 20, or 30 years), and the company is responsible for investing the extra funds paid in during the early years to cover the increasing costs in the later years (level term). It is up to the company to manage this, and they are responsible for paying the death benefit during the term of the insurance, irrespective of whether they made money or not. Each of the 50 state departments of insurance closely regulate and watch each company, and take over failing companies so the guarantees to the policy holders are secure. Technically, guarantees are limited to the claims-paying ability of the company. In actuality, "A" rated companies do not default because of the close regulation, and the state's ability and willingness to take over a weak company, and sell it to a strong one.

Technically, an annually renewable term policy can be renewed forever, but the increases in premiums each year eventually make it unaffordable. A level term policy will only have an increase after the entire term is completed, at which time there is a huge increase in premium, which usually makes it unaffordable. This is why you want to choose the exact term of the policy when you buy it to match your projected needs in the future.

If you feel that you are still going to need coverage in thirty years, you are generally better off buying a "permanent" policy, which offers you less death benefit for the same premium initially, but usually continuous flat premiums over time, except as described below.

Whole Life (WL):
1. Your premiums never change.
2. There is a guaranteed cash value.
3. There is a guaranteed death benefit.

4. The growth rate of the value is modest and consistent.
5. The growth of the death benefit and cash value purely depends on the overall profitability of the company, paid to policy owners as dividends. While there is no guarantee that there will be dividends every year, if you buy from a highly rated company that has paid dividends for the past 50, 75, or 150 years, it is not unreasonable to expect that they will continue to do so.

Universal Life (UL):

1. Premiums can change; either by your choice (depending on if you have the cash to pay them or not), by the company's choice (if the policy is performing poorly, and higher premiums are needed to keep it in force), or the death benefit can be reduced so that the premiums are adequate to fund the policy.
2. Cash value can go to zero.
3. Death benefit can go to zero (and the policy expires).
4. The growth rate of the value can vary, from 2% and up, and generally can change once a year (but not go below 2%). Gains are locked in every year—once they go up, they cannot go below that level, but that can be capped at a pre-determined annual maximum.
5. Interest, not dividends, is used to fuel policy value growth. Interest can be zero, unless a rider is purchased to guarantee some minimal level of interest.

Guaranteed Universal Life (GUL):

1. Similar to Universal Life (above) but the death benefit is guaranteed at a certain amount.

Indexed Universal Life (IUL):

The main difference between plain Universal Life (above) and Indexed Universal Life is that with IUL, the growth of the value of the policy is tied to a market index, like the S&P 500 or similar. Your premiums are not actually invested in the market (the company chooses how to invest), but your growth rate is determined by the index, and not interest rates. This rate can be as low as 0% (no growth). Gains are locked in every year—once they go up, they cannot go below that level, but that can be capped at a pre-determined annual maximum.

Variable Universal Life (VUL):

1. Premiums can change, either by your choice (depending on if you have the cash to pay them or not) or by the company's choice (if the policy is performing poorly, and higher premiums are needed to keep it in force).
2. Cash value can go to zero.
3. Death benefit can go to zero (and the policy expires).
4. The growth rate of the value can vary, or actually decrease, year to year.
5. Returns on funds that your money is invested in determine the growth rate (or loss rate). You get to choose the funds, and have the right to switch them, but the performance is the same as if you had invested directly in them in a brokerage account. There are fees associated with each fund, and there is a fee associated with managing the account, even though no one (but you) is looking over your allocations and making recommendations. Gains are NOT locked in every year—once they go up, they can go down below that level, depending on the index. It is as if you invested in those funds outside the insurance policy. The upside is that gains are not capped. The downside is that you pay more in fees than if you invested in those funds directly, without hiring a financial advisor.

A key difference between all of these "permanent" policies and Whole Life is that if the underlying indexes or interest rates do not hold up to projections, the policies could be worth a lot less than originally illustrated, or become worthless altogether. The risk is shifted from the insurance company to the insured. With Whole Life, the worst that could happen is just that the policyholder realizes the weaker, guaranteed performance. (Note: this rarely happens with "A" rated companies. What usually happens is a return somewhere between the projected and the guaranteed rate, and closer to the projected rate.) The risk stays with the insurance company.

Questions to Ask Yourself In Order to Select the Right Policy for You:

Do I need a death benefit for a given number of years, or for my entire lifetime? In other words, will it be okay if I die in twenty or thirty years, and there is no policy in force, or is it really important that no matter how old I am when I die, my heirs get a pay out? If you only need coverage for a certain number of years, a term policy will have the lowest premium cost. However, you are extremely likely to outlive the term, so you are extremely unlikely to ever collect a death benefit. Term policies are designed to mitigate the risk of dying too soon—they are not good for retirement or old age income.

Do I want to recover more than I pay in premiums, and am I willing to wait a decade or longer? If so, whole life or other "permanent" insurance may be preferred over term.

Who do I want to bear the risk of the policy living up to expectations— me, or the insurance company?

Am I just looking to make my money grow as fast as possible, and don't really care about death benefit? In this case, you probably don't want life insurance at all—you can invest money less expensively elsewhere.

ADDITIONAL RESOURCES, REFERENCES, AND ACKNOWLEDGEMENTS

"NOLHGA, the Life and Health Insurance Guaranty System, and the Financial Crisis of 2008-2009, " Peter G. Gallanis, President, NOLHGA, June 5, 2009

"The Disclosure Solution to the Problems Consumers Face in the Life Insurance Marketplace," R. Brian Fechtel, CFA, undated

Primary book editing provided by Kyle Ashcraft. To access his editing services, contact Kyle at KyleLAshcraft@gmail.com. He was indispensible to getting this book edited and organized. Each time he revisited the manuscript, it improved. (Note: I made the final revisions, so if you see errors, they are mine, and not his.)

Additional editing credit goes to Talia Smart, who can be reached at www.editingissmart.com. She proved valuable input to the both structure and details.

Cover design is by Enid Nolesco at enid@rawstorytelling.org. She is excellent at both design and branding, and extremely creative.

Interior layout is by Velin Saramov at perseusvelin@gmail.com.

Some of these people were resourced through Upwork.com

Made in the USA
Columbia, SC
23 January 2019